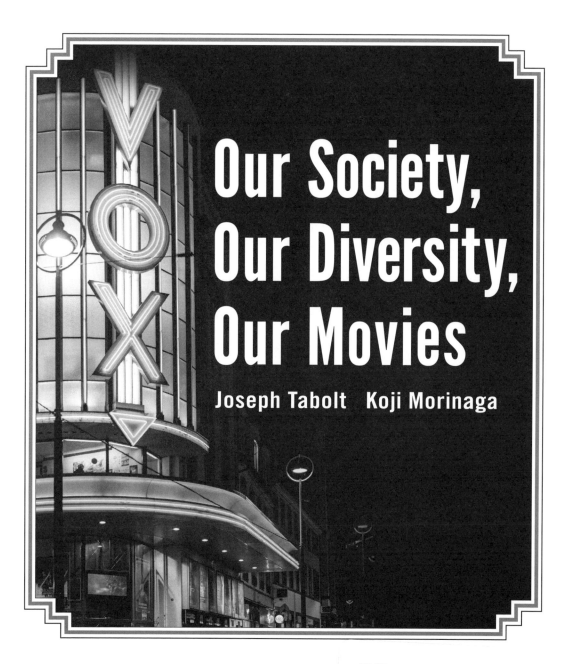

Our Society, Our Diversity, Our Movies

Joseph Tabolt   Koji Morinaga

JN033983

KINSEIDO

Kinseido Publishing Co., Ltd.
3-21 Kanda Jimbo-cho, Chiyoda-ku,
Tokyo 101-0051, Japan

First published 2020 by Kinseido Publishing Co., Ltd.

Cover design Takayuki Minegishi
Text design   guild
Photos   p.11 ©Laurence Agron/Dreamstime.com; p.17 ©Laurence Agron/Dreamstime.com, ©Blurf/
              Dreamstime.com; p.29 ©Dwong19/Dreamstime.com; p.35 ©Starstock/Dreamstime.com, ©Mircea
              Nicolescu/Dreamstime.com; p.41 ©Imagecollect/Dreamstime.com, ©Alexey Stiop/Dreamstime.com;
              p.47 ©Laurence Agron/Dreamstime.com, ©Erik Lattwein/Dreamstime.com; p.59 ©Featureflash/
              Dreamstime.com; p.65 ©Denis Makarenko/Dreamstime.com; p.71 ©Jaguarps/Dreamstime.com,
              ©David Fowler/Dreamstime.com; p.77 ©Featureflash/Dreamstime.com; p.83 ©Featureflash/
              Dreamstime.com; p.89 ©Featureflash/Dreamstime.com, ©Antonella865/Dreamstime.com; p.95
              ©Featureflash/Dreamstime.com

🎧 音声ファイル無料ダウンロード

https://www.kinsei-do.co.jp/download/4101

この教科書で 🎧 DL 00 の表示がある箇所の音声は、上記 URL または QR コードにて
無料でダウンロードできます。自習用音声としてご活用ください。

- ▶ PC からのダウンロードをお勧めします。スマートフォンなどでダウンロードされる場合は、
  ダウンロード前に「解凍アプリ」をインストールしてください。
- ▶ URL は、**検索ボックスではなくアドレスバー (URL 表示欄)** に入力してください。
- ▶ お使いのネットワーク環境によっては、ダウンロードできない場合があります。

⊙ **CD 00** 左記の表示がある箇所の音声は、教室用 CD（Class Audio CD）に収録されています。

Preface

Today, people and information circulate the globe freely, bringing with them new possibilities for innovation and problem-solving. However, to make these possibilities happen we must work together with people who see the world very differently from us. For this, when we evaluate the actions of others, we must not blindly reapply judgments about the world we have already made based on personal experiences. In a word, we must learn to recognize our prejudices and see past them, to discover new ways of seeing the world. In so doing, we will be able to not only understand others better but also come up with wonderfully creative ideas that would never occur to us if we could only see the world in one way.

This text features 15 movies, each of which portrays the lives of outstanding individuals who struggle to succeed due to the prejudices of others concerning their race, sexuality, religion, culture, social class, education, etc. Each essay attempts to show the problems these individuals face and the behavior they take in response, framed in their own perspectives. It is my hope that thinking about how these 15 outstanding individuals saw the world and how their perspective shaped their futures will serve as practice for understanding and cooperating with others in our increasingly diverse world.

Joseph Tabolt

はじめに

　本テキストは「多文化社会／多文化共生」をキーワードに、映画を来たるべき多文化社会のケーススタディ／モデルとして位置づけ、アカデミー賞受賞作から隠れた名作、知られざる傑作を通して多文化社会のありかたを学ぶことを企図したものである。本テキストの姉妹編にあたる *Our Time, Our Lives, Our Movies*（『映画で読むわたしたちの時代と社会』）では、有名なヒット映画15作品を取り上げ、主として映画と制作当時の社会情勢との相互関係を切り口とした。今回取り上げた映画はシリアスでかなり重い内容のものが多いが、扱われているテーマは学生の批判的思考力を鍛え、教養を深める上できわめて効果的なものばかりといえる。願わくは、学生には快・不快感だけを判断基準にせず、現実世界の厳しさや歴史にも目を向けて、現実に立脚した知性的な判断も織り交ぜた映画の評価を下してもらえればと思う。今回のテキストがその一助となれば幸いである。

森永弘司

Table of Contents

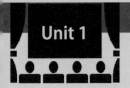

Unit 1

United by Desperation
"Three Billboards Outside Ebbing, Missouri"

自分が社会から疎外され、見下され、取り残されていると感じた場合、社会に対する無力感や絶望感はどのようなかたちを取り、どこへ向かうのでしょうか。*Three Billboards Outside Ebbing, Missouri* のケースを見てみましょう。

©Avalon/時事通信フォト

Key Vocabulary Match-up DL 002  CD1-02

次の 1 ～ 5 の意味に合うものを a ～ e から選びましょう。

1. authority   (　)   **a.** belonging to the countryside
2. billboard   (　)   **b.** someone who lacks any positive qualities
3. racist   (　)   **c.** a large sign in a public place such as beside a
4. rural   (　)   road
5. trash   (　)   **d.** a social power to make others do what you say
                                     e. believing that a certain group is lesser than you

Reading

次の文を読みましょう。

    Few would argue the fact that "white Americans" are the dominant socioeconomic group in the US; they have the greatest media presence, social authority and financial resources. Nevertheless, not all Caucasian Americans
5 are allowed membership to this group; those who are deemed undereducated, poor, rural, uncivilized, or racist, are often put in an inferior group called "white trash." However, unlike groups which possess clear points in common such as race or religion, there is little solidarity
10 among the people grouped as "white trash." *Three Billboards Outside Ebbing, Missouri* depicts the struggles within the white trash group, particularly between protagonist Mildred and antagonist Dixon, and illustrates how desperation provides a scary point in common around
15 which former enemies can rally together.

    The protagonist, Mildred, is in many ways not typical white trash. Although she is poor, rural and bad-mannered, she runs her own business and counts Denise, a black woman she employs, as her best friend. Further-
20 more, though not formally educated, she has a razor-sharp wit and the ability to research information she needs. Her daughter was raped and murdered, but after five years the police have found nothing and, she believes, have forgotten the case. Insightfully judging that media presence
25 is the best way to get her demands met, she rents three billboards and prints offensive remarks on them, homing in on Willoughby, the widely respected chief of police. She is met with fierce opposition from many, but her plan to get her daughter's case back in the spotlight succeeds.
30 Despite this, in the end, the media changes sides and, watching her daughter's case fade out again, she learns that even fierce determination and resourceful thinking is not enough to get her needs addressed. Must she give

socioeconomic
社会経済的な

Caucasian 白色人種の

protagonist 主人公

antagonist 敵対者

Insightfully 洞察して

homing in on ... …に狙いを定める

resourceful 機知に富んだ

up all hope of vindication?

Dixon, although a member of the local police, starts
as a cookie-cutter example of white trash. He is racist and
seems incapable of logical reasoning. He is rumored to
have tortured a black man, often tries to show his authority when he is angry, even if there has been no crime com-
mitted, and is in general a laughing stock in the town. He
makes little effort to think out his actions, usually acting
on emotional impulses. He is also a believer in authority
and blindly trusts the validity of his mother and Chief
Willoughby. Needless to say, Mildred, who has attacked
Willoughby and the authority of the police in general, is
his arch enemy. However, Willoughby's death transforms
Dixon; Dixon decides to try thinking for himself. This
leads to an almost immediate disillusionment with the
police. Forced to recognize that his hitherto blind faith in
authority could no longer serve as his guide, Dixon is left
with no avenue to choose his next move. What can he do
to satisfy his need to bring justice?

Ultimately, Dixon and Mildred, despite their initial
disgust for one another, are united through their desperation. Without education, social authority, or financial
means, neither of them has the resources to achieve their
goals. Instead, they band together in anger toward a society which has abandoned them, forming a union with no
real purpose other than to validate their anger. As Mildred says at the end of the movie about their plan of action as she and Dixon ride off into the horizon, "I guess we
can decide along the way." In spite of the deceptively
bright tone of the last scene, the reality is horrific. Determined to fulfill some ill-defined sense of justice, we can
only wonder what drastic, misguided measures they may
take on the way.

vindication 正しいことの
　証明

laughing stock 笑いもの

think out ...
　...を考え抜く

arch enemy 宿敵

disillusionment
　幻滅、失望
hitherto これまで

validate
　正当性を立証する

deceptively 一見すると

Comprehension Check

Read & Write

次の質問が本文の内容に合えば T（True）を、合わなければ F（False）を選びましょう。
また、その理由を本文から抜き出してみましょう。

1. "White trash" is a group just like any other.　　　　　　　T / F

Why?: _____

2. Dixon is very loyal to people in positions of power.　　　　T / F

Why?: _____

3. Mildred and Dixon's hopeless situation makes it difficult for them to get along.

　　　　　　　　　　　　　　　　　　　　　　　　　　　　T / F

Why?: _____

Listen & Write　　　　🎧 DL 007~009　◎ CD1-07 ~ ◎ CD1-09

音声を聞いて空所を埋めてから、本文の内容に最も合うものを選びましょう。

1. _____ does Mildred decide to _____ three billboards?

(A) She is angry about her daughter.

(B) She wants the world to know about her daughter.

(C) She wants to express her feelings.

(D) She is white trash.

2. _____ is the basis for most of Dixon's _____?

(A) Reason

(B) Resources

(C) Emotion

(D) Authority

3. _____ is the motivation for Dixon and Mildred's _____?

(A) They disgust one another.

(B) They want to justify their feelings.

(C) They have no other choice.

(D) They want to change society.

Write & Speak

次の語句の意味を英英辞典で調べて書いてみましょう。その後で、ペアを組んで相手に説明してみましょう。

> **A:** "white trash" means

> **B:** "desperate" means

Thinking about Our Diversity

次の質問について考えて、自分の意見を書いてみましょう。ペアやグループで話し合ってもかまいません。

1. Imagine that you are "white trash." What would you do about your feelings of powerlessness and hopelessness toward society? Also, how do you think you would feel toward more economically privileged social groups?

_____

_____

_____

_____

2. Imagine that you belong to some economically privileged social group. How would you treat white trash? How would you interpret their frustration?

_____

_____

_____

_____

Three Billboards Outside Ebbing, Missouri（2017）
『スリー・ビルボード』

本作は第90回アカデミー賞で作品賞・脚本賞など6部門にノミネートされ、主人公ミルドレッドを演じたフランシス・マクドーマンドが『ファーゴ』（96）に続いて2度目となる主演女優賞を受賞。また、ディクソン巡査を演じたサム・ロックウェルが助演男優賞を受賞した。

ミズーリ州とプアホワイト

　『スリー・ビルボード』の原題 *Three Billboards Outside Ebbing, Missouri* が示すように、この映画においてミズーリ州は背景として重要な役割を果たしている（ちなみに Ebbing は架空の町である）。ミズーリ州はアメリカの中西部に位置する州で、キリスト教の信仰があつい「バイブル・ベルト」（Bible belt：聖書地帯）と呼ばれる地帯に含まれている。したがって、キリスト教保守派の影響力が強く、教会の数も多い。日曜日に教会に出席する人が多く、かつては進化論を教えることが禁止されていた。州の人口の8割弱が白人で、1割弱が黒人、その他はヒスパニック系、アジア系、ネイティブ・アメリカンおよびミックスである。いまだに人種差別が根強く残っており、2014年には18歳の黒人青年が白人の警官によって射殺された事件をめぐって抗議行動が起こり、暴動や略奪に発展した。

　この映画には「プアホワイト」（poor white）あるいは「ホワイトトラッシュ」（white trash）、「レッドネック」（red neck）と呼ばれる、差別的で暴力的で、女性を侮蔑する貧しい白人たちが登場する。また、アメリカの経済成長から取り残された低賃金で働く白人は、ミズーリ州やバージニア州では「ヒルビリー」（hillbilly：山地に暮らす人）、南部のフロリダ州や  ジョージア州では「クラッカー」（cracker）と呼ばれる。この映画の主要登場人物であるディクソン巡査も教養にかけるレイシストで、女性を蔑視する典型的なヒルビリーである。加えて、彼はこの地では特に忌避され差別視されている同性愛者であることを暗示するような描かれ方もされている。

　本作の見所のひとつは、尊敬する上司のウィロビー署長の遺言によってディクソンが大きく変身を果たすところにある。ウィロビーは解雇されて自暴自棄になっていたディクソンに宛てた遺書で "But what you need to become a detective ... is Love. Because thru Love comes Calm, and thru Calm comes Thought. ... You don't even need a gun. And you definitely don't need Hate."（警察官にとって最も重要なのは、愛だ。愛は平静を導き、平静は思考を導く。（中略）拳銃は要らない。憎しみも要らない）と語りかける。この言葉によって憎しみの人から愛する人へと変貌を遂げたディクソンは、主人公ミルドレッドの娘を殺害したと思われる人物の DNA を命懸けで採取する。そして映画はこの男をアイダホ州に探しに行くディクソンの車にミルドレッドが同乗する場面で幕が閉じられるのである。

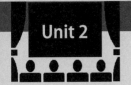

Unit 2

Assigning a Label
"Moonlight"

自分らしく生きるとはどういうことでしょうか。人生とは、他人との関係の中で時に自分を見失い、そして自分を再発見する旅のようなものといえるかもしれません。*Moonlight* の主人公 Chiron はどのような旅をするか見てみましょう。

©Collection Christophel

 Key Vocabulary Match-up    DL 010   CD1-10

次の 1 ～ 5 の意味に合うものを a ～ e から選びましょう。

1. assign   (   )

2. characteristics (   )

3. expectation   (   )

4. individual   (   )

5. prejudice   (   )

a. something you believe will be true or happen

b. belonging to a particular person

c. to give a person a particular duty

d. the distinguishing features of someone or something

e. often negative beliefs or actions toward the members of a group without considering each case

次の文を読みましょう。

"In moonlight, black boys look blue. You blue, that's what I'm gon' call you. 'Blue'." As the old woman quoted in this line from *Moonlight* did, we all assign labels to others based on fragmentary aspects of them, for example, "gay" for homosexuals and "black" for black-skinned individuals of African descent. In addition, since they are based on only fragments of an individual, a single individual can receive any number of labels. Further confusing matters, our prejudice leads us to attribute additional, often unfavorable, characteristics to the labels and expect people to behave according to the assumptions that go with the labels we give them. Whether or not our expectations are correct, they put pressure on others to try to fit them and thereby influence who they are. Finding a sense of self while trying to live up to the expectations of those around us is a difficult and confusing task. *Moonlight* guides us through the self-searching quest of Chiron, who all the while must face questions such as, "Am I a faggot?," "Am I Black?," "Am I soft?," "Am I little?" and finally, "Am I me?"

Chiron struggles throughout his life to find himself among the various demands on his character from others. With an effeminate way of walking, young Chiron's behavior does not fit in with the typical "black boys." The other black boys cast him out, sometimes calling him "Little" and sometimes "faggot." Following their expectations, he acts timidly, stays out of class activities and becomes the go-to target for school bullies. Meanwhile, Juan, his guardian and role-model, encourages a confused and unhappy Chiron: "You're not a faggot. You can be gay, but you don't have to let nobody call you a faggot." To escape the "faggot" label, Chiron rebuilds himself in a new location away from all the people of his childhood. Modeling himself after Juan, he becomes what he thought a "fag-

gon' going to の主にアメリカの黒人英語の方言

fragmentary 断片的な

sense of self 自意識、自我
live up to ... …に応える、…に沿う

all the while ずっと

faggot （侮蔑的に）男性同性愛者

effeminate 男らしくない

cast out ... …を追放する、…をのけ者にする

go-to target 格好の的

model after ... …を手本とする

got" is not: a strong lone wolf, and a drug dealer. However,
35 *Moonlight* also presents a more positive kind of label.

Chiron's only childhood best friend, Kevin, had a different label for him: Black. This was important because unlike "faggot" or even "gay," Kevin assigned this label to Chiron based on his individual feelings for him. In fact, it
40 symbolizes Kevin's expectations of Chiron at odds with those of the other children. When Kevin meets adult Chiron over 10 years later, he asks "Who is you, Chiron?" Although Kevin has changed his label to "Chiron," the muscles, the gold accessories and certainly Chiron being a
45 drug dealer were not characteristics he would have assigned to it. As a result of his focus on not being a faggot, Chiron has also stopped being what his loved ones expected. After his reunion with Kevin, we are left with hope that Chiron may find self-fulfillment, guided by the loving expectations of Kevin for "Chiron" rather than a desire to fit in with or escape from some generalized label.

If we are careful, generalized labels can be useful in helping groups of individuals with a common need. Priority seating in the train is only possible if we have individuals we label "elderly" or "handicapped." Likewise, before a discussion of gay rights can exist, there must first be a recognizable group of gay people. Nevertheless, very few are happy having their identity dictated by such a label, whether it be "gay," "straight," "white," or "black." Essentially, we can look at Chiron as a case study of the harmful effects of these when applied to individuals. His story also demonstrates the guidance we can gain when we lose our own paths from individualized labels placed on us by well-meaning loved ones. We all have times when we need
65 a Kevin in our lives.

at odds with ...
…と相容れない、
…と対立して

loved one 最愛の人

self-fulfillment 自己実現

dictate
命令する、指示する

well-meaning 善意の

Comprehension Check

Read & Write

次の質問が本文の内容に合えば T（True）を、合わなければ F（False）を選びましょう。
また、その理由を本文から抜き出してみましょう。

1. Labels we put on others are often influenced by our prejudice.　　　T / F

Why?: _____

2. Chiron pursued his ideal self throughout his life.　　　T / F

Why?: _____

3. Labels such as "handicapped" and "gay" are useful in understanding and helping specific individuals.　　　T / F

Why?: _____

Listen & Write　　　🎧 DL 015~017　　◉ CD1-15 ~ ◉ CD1-17

音声を聞いて空所を埋めてから、本文の内容に最も合うものを選びましょう。

1. _____ is often the _____ when someone has poor expectations of others?
(A) They act timidly.
(B) They ignore us.
(C) They change their behavior.
(D) They become enemies of society.

2. _____ does Chiron become a _____ _____?
(A) He wanted to meet Juan's expectations.
(B) He wanted to be like Juan.
(C) He admired drug dealers.
(D) He needed money.

3. _____ would an individual be dissatisfied if they were _____?
(A) They do not like the person who labeled them.
(B) They think the label is too general.
(C) They do not like the pressure that comes with it.
(D) They never label others.

Write & Speak

次の語句の意味を英英辞典で調べて書いてみましょう。その後で、ペアを組んで相手に説明してみましょう。

> **A:** "LGBT" means

> **B:** "gay" means

🎥 Thinking about Our Diversity

次の質問について考えて、自分の意見を書いてみましょう。ペアやグループで話し合ってもかまいません。

1. Imagine that you are a member of the LGBT community. Would you tell your friends? If you did, how would you say it? How would you want your friends to respond?

   _____

   _____

   _____

   _____

2. Imagine that your friend is a member of the LGBT community and has confessed this to you. How would you respond? How would you treat that friend in the future?

   _____

   _____

   _____

   _____

Moonlight（2016）
『ムーンライト』

本作は第89回アカデミー賞で8部門にノミネートされ、LGBTを扱った映画として史上初めて作品賞を受賞したほか、助演男優賞・脚色賞を受賞。フアン（Juan）を演じたマハーシャラ・アリは2年後に『グリーンブック』で再び助演男優賞を受賞している。

| Column | 『ムーンライト』の主人公が抱える3つの差別 |

　『ムーンライト』の主人公であるシャロンは3つの差別の中で生きている。1つは黒人差別であり、以前に比べると露骨な差別は少なくなったとはいえ、黒人に対する差別意識はアメリカ社会に厳として存在している。同時に、白人社会の中にもヒエラルキーは存在しており、アメリカ社会の指導者の多くはWASPに属する人々である。WASPとはWhite Anglo-Saxon Protestantの略で、今日その優位性はかなり揺らいでいるとはいえ、依然として政財界の指導者にはWASP出身者が多い。

　2つ目の差別は黒人社会内部での差別である。黒人社会にも上流、中流、下流という社会階層が存在する。シャロンの住む家は、黒人の中でも主として貧困層が暮らすスラム街にあり、シャロンの母のように薬物依存者が多く住み、売春も珍しくない犯罪多発地区で、きわめて治安の悪い場所である（映画の舞台はフロリダ州マイアミに設定されている）。したがって、黒人社会の中でも最も差別されることが多い地区であるといえる。

　シャロンはこの貧民街にある学校でfaggot（俗語でホモ、オカマの意味）と呼ばれていじめにあうが、同性愛者であるということがシャロンの抱える3つ目の差別の理由である。近年、性的少数者（セクシュアル・マイノリティ）を指す言葉としてLGBTという言葉を目にする機会が多くなっているが、これは、Lesbian（レズビアン、女性同性愛者）、Gay（ゲイ、男性同性愛者）、Bisexual（バイセクシュアル、両性愛者）、Transgender（トランスジェンダー、出生時に診断された性と自認する性の不一致）の頭文字を取って作られた略語である。また、LGBTがすべての性的少数者を網羅しているわけではないために、Asexual（アセクシュアル、同性にも異性にも性的欲望を持たない人）のA、Intersex（インターセックス、身体的に男女の区別がつきにくい人）のI、Questioning（クエスチョニング、自分の性別や性的指向に確信が持てない人）のQなど、LGBT以外のカテゴリーの性的少数者を表す単語の頭文字をLGBTにつけることもある。

　『ムーンライト』はLGBTを扱った映画として初めてアカデミー賞作品賞を受賞したことで話題になったが、この映画の素晴らしさは、3重の差別を抱えるシャロンが、父親代わりの存在ともいうべきフアンと親友ケビンとの交流を通して自己実現を果たしていくところにこそあるといえよう。

Unit 3

Prejudice and Egocentrism

"Hidden Figures"

1960 年代初頭のアメリカにはまだ人種差別が色濃く残り、それに加えて女性に対する差別もありました。*Hidden Figures* はそのような時代背景の中で、自ら機会と平等を勝ち取った NASA に勤務する実在の女性たちの物語です。

©Collection Christophel

Key Vocabulary Match-up

 DL 018　CD1-18

次の 1 〜 5 の意味に合うものを a 〜 e から選びましょう。

1. contribution　　(　　)

2. overcome　　　(　　)

3. privileged　　　(　　)

4. tendency　　　 (　　)

5. unconscious　　(　　)

a. having rights or resources not available to others

b. an act that helps achieve some goal

c. to defeat a problem or obstacle

d. being present in one's thoughts or actions but un-noticed

e. something that is likely to happen or be done based on past happenings

次の文を読みましょう。

We all have unconscious prejudices. Often, prejudice is a result not of dislike for another person or group of people, but of a lazy tendency by privileged individuals to fail to notice that they are privileged or, alternatively, to
5 accept things the way they are. *Hidden Figures* follows the paths of three remarkable black women suffering from double discrimination in the 1960s, which discriminates along both gender and racial lines. Their stories illustrate the great effort typically needed to make those in
10 privilege act and are a call to action to its viewers to consider more carefully the situations of others before passing judgment.

call to action
行動への呼びかけ
pass judgment 批判する

Katherine Johnson, a gifted mathematician, is an asset to NASA but she is taken for granted by her boss, Al
15 Harrison. She is a black woman and faces severe disadvantages compared to her white male colleagues. On her first day, she asks a female white colleague where the bathroom is. She is informed, "Sorry. I have no idea where your bathroom is." She finds it is 40 minutes away! De-
20 spite such difficulties, she makes great contributions to the spaceflight program. One day, Al notices that she is often on break for a long time. He scolds her based on his reasonable expectation that NASA employees should be dedicated and therefore not take long breaks. This gives
25 Katherine the perfect chance to show him and all of the other white males in the room just how privileged they are. After this, Al abolishes colored bathrooms. Katherine's hard work and genius overcame Al's egocentricity.

egocentricity
自己中心（性）

Another main character, Dorothy Vaughan, is a born
30 team leader, but her career is also hindered by her blackness. Dorothy does the work of a manager, but administration will not create a manager position for her team. Vivian Mitchel, her immediate superior and a white fe-

male, passively accepts this poor treatment of Dorothy as
35 the way things are. Later, when Dorothy finds out that
human calculators will be replaced by computers, she
teaches herself and her team to program computers. Thus,
she secures a new position for her team on the computers.
Seeing this, Vivian wants to send her team of white calcu-
40 lators to Dorothy for training, but Dorothy cannot agree
because she is not a manager. Vivian claims she has nothing against Dorothy or any black person. Dorothy merely
comments, "I know that you probably believe that." Soon
enough, Vivian announces that Dorothy is now the official
45 manager of her team. Dorothy's quick work forced Vivian
to abandon her passive stance and advocate for Dorothy.

Hidden Figures tells the story of remarkable black
American women who work their way up in NASA in
times when the law did not give equal rights to blacks or
50 women. However, the central theme of this movie is not
civil rights, but the lazy tendency of privileged individuals to disregard the difficulties borne by others. What en-
ables these women to succeed is not changes to the law,
but their exceptional talent. This allowed them to assume
55 essential roles. As a result, individuals in privilege had no
choice but to realize that passively accepting segregation
was counterproductive; segregation was preventing the
women from making the great contributions of which
they were capable.

60 Is a society where a person must be exceptionally talented before we acknowledge the difficulties they face re-
ally acceptable? This is a two-way message to all of us. As
Al and Vivian eventually did, we must take another look
around us and think about the challenges others might
65 be facing. Otherwise, we may misjudge those around us
entirely. Likewise, as Katherine and Dorothy did, we
must vocalize our predicament when we are at a disad-
vantage, as the privileged may have simply not thought
about it.

human calculators
計算手

work one's way up
出世する、登りつめる

civil rights 公民権

borne by ... …が負担する

have no choice but to
... …するしかない

counterproductive
逆効果の、非生産的な

vocalize 声を上げる
predicament 苦境

Comprehension Check

Read & Write

次の質問が本文の内容に合えば T（True）を、合わなければ F（False）を選びましょう。
また、その理由を本文から抜き出してみましょう。

1. Katherine works under the same conditions as the rest of her NASA colleagues.

T / F

Why?: _____

2. At first, Vivian thinks that it is better to segregate black women.　　T / F

Why?: _____

3. Privileged individuals do their best to recognize the disadvantages of those around them.　　T / F

Why?: _____

Listen & Write

DL 024~026　CD1-24 ～ CD1-26

音声を聞いて空所を埋めてから、本文の内容に最も合うものを選びましょう。

1. _____ was the initial factor for Al to _____ his self-centered thinking?
(A) Careful thought
(B) Katherine's unfair situation
(C) Katherine's potential
(D) New rules at NASA

2. _____ does Vivian probably _____ according to Dorothy?
(A) She personally is not prejudiced.
(B) She does not treat black women differently.
(C) She is fighting for black rights.
(D) She is Dorothy's friend.

3. _____ did NASA _____ its segregation policy?
(A) Moral reform
(B) The law
(C) The need to produce better results
(D) Katherine and Dorothy's complaints

Write & Speak

次の語句の意味を英英辞典で調べて書いてみましょう。その後で、ペアを組んで相手に説明してみましょう。

A: "discrimination" means

B: "segregation" means

 Thinking about Our Diversity

次の質問について考えて、自分の意見を書いてみましょう。ペアやグループで話し合ってもかまいません。

1. Imagine that you were treated unfairly just because you were male or female and a member of a different race. How would that make you feel? What would you do in such a situation?

_____

_____

_____

_____

2. Imagine that you were prejudiced against someone because of their sex and race. How would you react if one of those people pointed your prejudice out to you?

_____

_____

_____

_____

Hidden Figures（2016）
『ドリーム』

実在の NASA の女性たち（写真は主人公の 1 人であるキャサリン・ジョンソン）をもとにした本作は、第 89 回アカデミー賞で作品賞・助演女優賞・脚色賞にノミネートされた。日本公開時、宇宙開発をイメージさせるために『ドリーム　私たちのアポロ計画』という邦題が予定されていたが、アポロ計画ではなくマーキュリー計画を描いた映画であることから指摘を受け、『ドリーム』に変更された。

Column ## "Hidden Figures" というタイトルが示唆すること

　　『ドリーム』（原題 *Hidden Figures*）は、第二次世界大戦以降の東西冷戦下でアメリカとソ連が熾烈な宇宙開発競争を繰り広げていた 1961 年の NASA のラングレー研究所を舞台に、優秀な頭脳を持つ 3 人の黒人女性――幼い頃から数学の天才とみなされ、ロケットの打ち上げに欠かせない複雑な計算や解析に取り組むキャサリン・ジョンソン、新たに導入された IBM のコンピューターによるデータ処理の責任者に任命されるドロシー・ヴォーン、黒人女性初の NASA の航空宇宙エンジニアをめざすメアリー・ジャクソン――が「マーキュリー計画」と呼ばれる有人宇宙飛行計画の実現に貢献しようと奮闘する姿を描いている。

　　1961 年当時、アメリカの南部諸州（本作の舞台であるバージニア州も含まれる）では、主として黒人をターゲットにした「ジム・クロウ法」（Jim Crow laws）と呼ばれる州法が施行されていた。ジム・クロウとは 1828 年にケンタッキー州で上演されてヒットしたミュージカルの黒人の登場人物の名前で、後に黒人の蔑称と

なり、人種隔離制度にも用いられるようになった。ジム・クロウ法は、黒人を「奴隷ではないが白人よりも下の存在として隷属させる」ための法律であり、黒人たちは交通機関、学校や図書館などの公共機関、ホテルやレストランやバー、さらには水飲み場やトイレでも "colored" の表示がある場所や席しか使用できなかった。

　　こうした人種差別にもとづく人種隔離法の撤廃と、黒人の公民権獲得を求めて精力的に活動したのがマーティン・ルーサー・キング・ジュニア（1929-68）である。彼はリンカーンの奴隷解放宣言 100 周年を記念する大集会を仲間たちと計画し、1963 年 8 月 28 日に首都ワシントンで 20 万人を超える参加者と大行進をおこなった。このときにリンカーン記念堂の前でおこなったのが、有名な "I Have a Dream" を含む演説である。キングやその他の公民権運動家の努力が実を結び、1964 年 7 月 2 日に公民権法（Civil Rights Act）が成立し、ジム・クロウ法は即時停止になった。

　　この映画が公開されるまで、ごく少数の人々にしかこの 3 人の黒人女性の存在が知られておらず、長らく "Hidden Figures"（知られざる人物たち）として封印されてきたのはなぜだろうか。その理由の一端は、当時の NASA のみならず、現在に至るも存在する白人や黒人といった人種を問わない性差別（女性差別）にあるであろう。『ドリーム』は人種と性別という二重の差別にも関わらず、自らの夢を実現した 3 人の黒人女性にスポットライトを当てた感動的な作品である。

Unit 4

— Slavery Systems

Human vs. Property

"12 Years A Slave"

奴隷制度は人間から自由や尊厳を奪い「物」として所有しようとする行為です。*12 Years A Slave* の主人公で実在の人物である Solomon も理不尽にすべてを奪われ奴隷とされました。彼は人間らしさを最後まで失わずにいられるでしょうか。

©Photo12

 Key Vocabulary Match-up   DL 027   ⊙ CD1-27

次の１～５の意味に合うものをａ～ｅから選びましょう。

1. attempt   (   )   **a.** the things that a person owns

2. belongings   (   )   **b.** something you decide to do before other things

3. painful   (   )   **c.** a person who must obey another person but is not

4. priority   (   )   paid

5. slave   (   )   **d.** highly unpleasant, physically or emotionally

                                  e. an act trying to achieve something

次の文を読みましょう。

　Imagine you own a robot that can do everything a human can do and whose only goal is to carry out your orders. It does not have other priorities like family, friends, or personal values, no desire for leisure time, not even
5　any feelings that you have to worry about hurting. Surely anyone would want to claim such a useful thing as their property. Slavery systems are an attempt to create such property by making humans the property of other humans. Of course, legally enslaving a human is not enough
10　to change them into property, so slave owners created systems to break them in. The painful life of Solomon Northup, the protagonist of *12 Years A Slave*, shows us that such a system can never truly succeed.

　Solomon was living a free life just like us. He played
15　the fiddle for a living, had a family he loved and had friends and acquaintances around his town. One day, however, he was kidnapped and enslaved. From then on, a process to erase his free will, his scholarship, his creative potential, his ability to plan for the future and ev-
20　erything that made him human began. The first step was to make him verbally say he was a slave. He was brutally whipped, robbed of all belongings, and forced to take on a new name. Having lost everything from his life, he indeed began to verbally admit that he was a slave.

25　The next step was to make him forget his education and creative ability. At one point, Solomon creates a solution to getting over a river on the plantation and the plantation owner is greatly pleased. However, soon after, a plantation carpenter hangs him from a rope and nearly
30　kills him for saying his orders were inadequate. This teaches him to actively deny having any education or ability to think of new solutions. The last step was to make him give up his ability to have personal relation-

enslave 奴隷にする

break in ... …をならす、…を調教する
Solomon Northup ソロモン・ノーサップ（実在の人物。1807- 没年不明）

fiddle バイオリン

From then on それ以降

free will 自由意志
creative potential 創造的潜在能力

verbally 言葉の上で
brutally 残酷に、容赦なく
take on ... …を引き受ける、…を獲得する

personal relationships 人間関係

ships. Solomon and an enslaved woman helped each other
35 get a grip on their predicaments through heart-felt discussion, forming a deep bond. Nevertheless, by the orders
of his owner, he has to whip her until the skin on her back
comes off. He learns that relationships are dangerous for
those who are enslaved.

40   The process of breaking-in teaches Solomon that his
humanity, no matter how productive it may be, is a danger to his life as long as he belongs to another human. On
the surface, he does his best to hide it, but it never actually goes away. No matter what he says, he remembers
45 his name, his home, his education, his creative potential,
and his friends and family. All of the enslaved, whenever
they could get away with it, helped each other, sang together, mourned for one another, and shared advice. However, they were not entitled to make any plans for the fu-
50 ture; they were not allowed to "live," only "survive" and
this may be the cruelest fate a human could receive.

    The failure of the slavery system to make humans
into property gives testament to what it means to be human. Humans cannot be "broken in" to become mere prop-
55 erty. We have an instinctive need to accumulate and share
knowledge, to discuss our world with one another and to
work towards a better world for ourselves to live in. But,
actually, what would you prefer—a piece of property
which can only do what you tell it to or a human ally who
60 can help you come up with new ideas and better solutions? It would seem that enslaving a human is, if anything, counterproductive.

get a grip on ...
　…を理解する、…を把握
　する

as long as ...
　…であるかぎり
On the surface 表面上は

get away with it
　処罰を免れる

testament 証拠

instinctive 本能的な

if anything
　どちらかといえば

Comprehension Check

Read & Write

次の質問が本文の内容に合えば T（True）を、合わなければ F（False）を選びましょう。
また、その理由を本文から抜き出してみましょう。

1. The slavery system succeeded in the first step with regards to Solomon. T / F

Why?: _____

2. Slaves were successfully trained to not have personal bonds with one another.

T / F

Why?: _____

3. A human would be the ideal worker if he/she could be turned into property.

T / F

Why?: _____

Listen & Write

DL 033~035　　CD1-33 ～ CD1-35

音声を聞いて空所を埋めてから、本文の内容に最も合うものを選びましょう。

1. _____ process best describes "_____ _____"?
   (A) Making humans forget their past
   (B) Whipping and physically abusing humans
   (C) Taking all the belongings of humans
   (D) Kidnapping and enslaving humans

2. _____ does Solomon _____ _____ his owner ideas?
   (A) His owner punishes him.
   (B) A white worker on the planation severely hurts him.
   (C) He decides he does not want to help his owners.
   (D) He forgets his education.

3. _____ did Solomon's _____ succeed in making Solomon do?
   (A) Forget his creativity
   (B) Give up surviving
   (C) Give up interpersonal relationships
   (D) Stop planning for the future

Write & Speak

次の語句の意味を英英辞典で調べて書いてみましょう。その後で、ペアを組んで相手に説明してみましょう。

> **A:** "property" means

> **B:** "humanity" means

🎥 Thinking about Our Diversity

次の質問について考えて、自分の意見を書いてみましょう。ペアやグループで話し合ってもかまいません。

1. Imagine that you are a slave. What part of yourself would you try to defend until the end? How would you try to keep your humanity? How would you feel toward your owner?

_____

_____

_____

_____

2. Imagine that you are a slave owner. How would you treat your slaves? Do you think you would feel any guilt about owning slaves? What do you think makes humans want to own other humans?

_____

_____

_____

_____

12 Years A Slave（2013）
『それでも夜は明ける』

実話をもとに19世紀のアメリカにおける奴隷時代を描いた本作は、第86回アカデミー賞で監督賞・主演男優賞・助演男優賞など9部門にノミネートされ、作品賞、助演女優賞、脚色賞を受賞した。

Column アメリカにおける黒人奴隷の歴史

　『それでも夜は明ける』は実話にもとづく映画であり、主人公ソロモン・ノーサップ（1807- 没年不明）は1841年にワシントンD.C.で誘拐され奴隷として売られてから筆舌に尽くしがたい苦難の日々を耐え、妻と子どもたちと再会を果たすことができたのは12年後の1853年のことであった。

　ソロモンが生きていた当時の首都ワシントンは奴隷制を採用し、奴隷売買も合法で、国内の奴隷貿易の中心地であった。ソロモンは誘拐されるまでは「自由黒人」（free negro）としてニューヨーク州のサラトガで暮らしていた。アメリカ文学者の宮津多美子氏によると、自由黒人とは「奴隷制廃止までに南部および北部諸州において自由人として（自由人の母親から）生まれた黒人もしくは北部における奴隷制廃止後に法的に自由となった黒人」と定義づけられている。アメリカ独立戦争（1775-83）の際、イギリス軍と植民地軍は黒人を軍隊に入れて戦った。多くが奴隷の身分だった黒人は、戦争に参加する代わりに自由身分を保証された。その結果、自由身分の黒人の数は戦後6万人に達した。南北戦争（1861-65）の前には、自由身分の黒人の数は全黒人の人口の1割を超えるようになった。ただし、自由黒人は白人と同等の自由が保障されていたわけではない。「フリーペーパー」と呼ばれる自由身分の証明書を常に携帯する必要があり、携帯しない黒人は奴隷とみなされるという慣行があった。

　アメリカ初の黒人奴隷は、1619年8月にバージニア植民地のジェームズタウンにオランダ商人に連れてこられ、タバコプランテーションの経営者に売り渡された20人の黒人であるといわれている。黒人をアフリカからアメリカに運ぶ奴隷船の船内環境はきわめて劣悪で、黒人1人に許された空間は寝返りを打つことさえ困難な非常に狭いスペースであった。また、食事はイモ類、なた豆、バナナなどを粉状にした家畜の餌に等しいものであった。

　アメリカがイギリスから独立した1776年には黒人奴隷の数は75万人に達していた。独立戦争の指導者でアメリカの初代大統領となるジョージ・ワシントン（1732-99）や「独立宣言」の起草者であるトーマス・ジェファーソン（1743-1826）は、独立宣言冒頭の "All men are created equal" という有名な文言で万人の平等を標榜していたにもかかわらず、自分たちが経営する農園では黒人奴隷を使役していた。「すべての人間」の中には、黒人は含まれていなかったわけである。南北戦争が終結し、憲法修正第13条によって奴隷制度が法的に廃止された1865年の時点では、黒人奴隷の数は400万人にまで達していた。

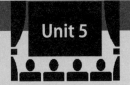

Unit 5

Choosing a Home

"Brooklyn"

Brooklyn の主人公 Eilis は仕事を求めてアイルランドからニューヨークへ移民としてやってきます。彼女の苦悩や葛藤を通して、私たちにとって祖国あるいは故郷とは何なのかを考えてみましょう。

©Avalon/時事通信フォト

Key Vocabulary Match-up DL 036  CD1-36

次の 1 ～ 5 の意味に合うものを a ～ e から選びましょう。

1. depression　　（　）　　**a.** a strong feeling of wanting something or someone

2. establish　　（　）　　**b.** to change one thing for another

3. location　　（　）　　**c.** a period of high unemployment and wide-spread poverty

4. longing　　（　）

5. replace　　（　）　　**d.** to form social or economic roots in a new area

　　　　　　　　　　　　　e. a place where something happens or exists

次の文を読みましょう。

We can all agree that everyone needs a place to call
"home." Home is where we are most ourselves. Even so, it
is surprisingly hard to pinpoint what makes somewhere a
good home. Most would agree that the location of our
5 home can change throughout our lives; perhaps our family moves, or perhaps we move out of our parents' house to
raise our own family. But, what about somewhere in a
different country with different customs or even a different language? In *Brooklyn*, the protagonist Eilis gives us
10 her answer to this question through her struggle to find a
place to call home in a foreign country.

Eilis is raised in Ireland during the depression in the
early 1950s. As a young adult, she is unable to find work
there, so she leaves for Brooklyn, NY, where her sister has
15 arranged a boarding house for her to live in and a job for
her. Once there, Eilis quickly discovers that just having a
place to sleep and a job does not make a place home. For
Eilis, home is where her family, particularly her sister, is.
In Brooklyn, she does not know the people around her
20 and the people around her do not know her. She does not
know the customs and at her residence she is surrounded
by strangers who, unlike her, are comfortable in Brooklyn
and with the rules of the house. Even at work, she is unable to make friendly chat with customers because she is
25 unfamiliar with the local sensibilities. All around, she
feels a sense of inferiority and alienation. Meanwhile,
whenever she reads her letters from her sister in Ireland
or hears Irish songs, she is overwhelmed with a longing
for "home." Eilis is suffering from homesickness.

30 However, she begins to grow new roots. She attends
an accounting class at Brooklyn University and earns
professional qualifications. She meets Tony, a kind Italian
boy and they fall in love at first sight. Eilis finds someone

pinpoint 正確に示す

boarding house 下宿

sensibility 感覚、感受性

inferiority 劣等（感）
alienation 疎外（感）

professional
 qualifications 職業資格

who, like her sister, thinks of her all the time and who
unconditionally appreciates her presence. After this, she
gains confidence in her surroundings, her performance at
work improves and she builds relationships of mutual
trust with her boarding mates. In short, she finds a place
in Brooklyn where she feels useful and wanted. Has
Brooklyn replaced Ireland as her home?

Suddenly, Eilis receives notice that her sister has
died. Eilis must choose: does she stay in Brooklyn and
continue her new life or does she go back to Ireland to
help her mother, who is now alone? When Tony lovingly
tells her to go and that "home is home," Eilis replies, "I'm
not sure I have a home anymore." Torn between two places, Eilis does not know what home is anymore. She goes
back, where her mother and childhood friend welcome
her. She is offered her sister's job as an accountant, and
even finds a suitable companion. Eilis is confronted with
a difficult decision. She has two places she can choose
from to call home. In the end, Eilis chooses Brooklyn over
her birthplace, showing us that the best home is not nec-
essarily the place we were born.

Brooklyn reflects an increasingly common trend in today's global society: it is often not the case that the people
who call a place home were born there, or even in that
country. The personal freedom we have in modern society
gives each of us the possibility to explore the world and
establish ourselves somewhere we truly feel needed and
at home. Eilis serves as an inspiration to all of us. She
gathered the courage to venture outside the place she had
always called home and find her way in a world filled with
opportunities. Ultimately, Eilis's journey led her to fulfill-
ment in a place far from her birth home.

unconditionally 無条件に

mutual trust 相互信頼

venture
危険を承知で試みる

Comprehension Check

Read & Write

次の質問が本文の内容に合えば T（True）を、合わなければ F（False）を選びましょう。
また、その理由を本文から抜き出してみましょう。

1. Eilis's relationship with Tony is similar to the one she has with her sister.　T / F

Why?: _____

2. For Eilis, Brooklyn and Ireland both seem like possible homes.　　　　T / F

Why?: _____

3. Most people think of a place as home because they were born and raised
there.　　　　　　　　　　　　　　　　　　　　　　　　　　　T / F

Why?: _____

Listen & Write

DL 042~044　CD1-42 ~ CD1-44

音声を聞いて空所を埋めてから、本文の内容に最も合うものを選びましょう。

1. _____ does Eilis _____ _____ Brooklyn instead of
_____ _____ her hometown?

(A) Her sister found a boarding house for her.

(B) She needed a job.

(C) She did not like her home.

(D) She did not know the customs there.

2. _____ best _____ Tony?

(A) Eilis's only marriage candidate

(B) A kind, French boy

(C) Eilis's support in Brooklyn

(D) Eilis's classmate at Brooklyn University

3. According to this essay, _____ is the most important characteristic of
a _____ _____?

(A) We feel needed there.

(B) We were born there.

(C) Our family is there.

(D) We have a job there.

Write & Speak

次の語句の意味を英英辞典で調べて書いてみましょう。その後で、ペアを組んで相手に説明してみましょう。

A: "home" means

B: "birthplace" means

🎥 Thinking about Our Diversity

次の質問について考えて、自分の意見を書いてみましょう。ペアやグループで話し合ってもかまいません。

1. Imagine you are an immigrant in a foreign country, find a job, make new friends and grow new roots there. In your personal opinion, could the country replace the country you were born in as your home?

2. Imagine you have to choose between the foreign country where you feel useful and wanted and the country you were born. Which would you choose and why?

Brooklyn（2015）
『ブルックリン』

アイルランドからニューヨークのブルックリンへ移民した若い女性エイリシュの葛藤を描いた本作は、第88回アカデミー賞で作品賞・主演女優賞・脚色賞にノミネートされた。エイリシュを演じたシアーシャ・ローナンの両親はアイルランド人で、本人もニューヨークに生まれアイルランドで育った。シアーシャ（Saoirse）という名前はアイルランド語で「自由」を意味する。

Column ／ **アイルランドとアイルランド系アメリカ人**

　『ブルックリン』の時代設定は1950年代初頭であるが、アイルランドは第二次世界大戦の際に中立を守ったために、アメリカの経済援助によって戦後ヨーロッパの復興を企図したマーシャル・プラン（Marshall Plan）から排除されていた。本作の主人公エイリシュのような若くて有能な女性がアイルランドで定職を得ることができなかったのも、国内の慢性的な不況が原因である。このような事情により、1950年代には多くのアイルランド人がアメリカに移住した。

　アイルランドは、前5世紀頃にヨーロッパ大陸から渡ってきたケルト人がもたらした文化とカトリック信仰をバックボーンとする国である。長年にわたり隣国イングランドの支配を受け、1649年にはイングランド議会軍を率いるオリバー・クロムウェルに征服されて植民地となった。以降、プロテスタントやイングランド国教会の人々から厳しい宗教的迫害を受け、数多くのアイルランドのカトリック教徒が命を奪われた。初期のアイルランド人移民がアメリカをめざしたのは宗教的迫害から逃れるためであり、特に19世紀初頭にカトリック系アイルランド人が集団的大移民を始めた。また、1845年から49年にかけて発生した「ジャガイモ飢饉」（potato famine）によって250万人以上のアイルランド人が祖国を離れ、その大部分がアメリカに移民した。この時にアメリカに移民したアイルランド人の中に、J・F・ケネディ大統領の曽祖父も含まれていたとのことである。

　さらに、1848年にカリフォルニアで金鉱が発見されたことで起こったゴールドラッシュがきっかけとなって、アイルランドからも多くの移民が押し寄せることとなった。ところが、アメリカ建国の立役者であったのはイギリスのプロテスタント派のピューリタン（清教徒）であり、アイルランド人はカトリックであるがゆえに差別されることが多く、たいていは雇用の安定しない危険な労働環境の仕事にしか就くことができなかった。20世紀初頭に建造されたタイタニック号の三等船室の乗客の大半はアメリカに向かう貧しいアイルランド移民で、船底のエンジンルームで汗だくになりながら働いていた労働者の多くもアイルランド人であったといわれている。

　その後、アイルランド系アメリカ人は様々な苦難に見舞われながらも奮闘努力を続け、アメリカで確固たる地位を獲得し、現在ではアメリカの総人口約2億6千万人のうちの4千万人にまで達している。

Unit 6
Be an Intercultural Interpreter
"Gran Torino"

あなたの家の隣に移民が引っ越してきたらどうしますか？ 自動車の街デトロイトに暮らす気難しい愛国主義者の老人である *Gran Torino* の主人公 Walt のケースを見てみましょう。

©Collection Christophel

Key Vocabulary Match-up 🎧 DL 045 💿 CD1-45

次の 1 ～ 5 の意味に合うものを a ～ e から選びましょう。

1. compromise	( )	**a.** being upsetting or rude
2. divide	( )	**b.** to assign a meaning to something
3. interpret	( )	**c.** to separate one unit into more than one
4. offensive	( )	**d.** to join together under a common purpose
5. unite	( )	**e.** to settle for less than your full wishes in order to reach an agreement

🎬 Reading

次の文を読みましょう。

What would you do if a foreign family with unfamiliar customs and a strange language moved in next to you? Would you try to befriend them or would you try to avoid them? Understanding one another's communication
5 styles is an important factor in making friends with someone, but this does not mean we cannot make friends with people from different cultures. *Gran Torino* gives a profound illustration of how communication style can divide groups which we traditionally consider part of the same
10 culture and unite groups with different cultures.

Walt Kowalski and his two sons are an instance of the divisive power of communication style. Walt, a veteran of the Korean War and a retired automobile technician, is a perfect example of traditional US masculinity. He sticks
15 with his opinion on what is right very stubbornly, he confronts others when he disagrees, he does not worry about hurting people's feelings and he uses very rough language. However, his sons belong to a new generation of Americans who often compromise their opinions, go to
20 great lengths to spare the feelings of others, and use very indirect language. Although Walt is their father and they have spent much of their lives together, they understand Walt's words on their own terms, interpreting them as indicative of his disappointment in them. Even their at-
25 tempt to celebrate his birthday results in a communication breakdown where both sides part ways unhappily. Neither Walt nor his sons take the time to notice the other's real intentions, and so their differences work as an unseen divisive force between them.

30 On the other hand, Sue, a street-wise Asian-American teenager and Walt's new neighbor, shows us how communication style can bring very different people together. Walt has many prejudices towards Asians due to his in-

befriend 友人になる

divisive 対立させる
veteran
　退役軍人、兵役経験者
Korean War
　朝鮮戦争（1950-53）
masculinity 男らしさ
stick with …
　…を堅持する、…にこだ
わる
stubbornly 頑固に

go to great lengths
　苦労を惜しまない
spare the feelings
　気持ちを思いやる

on one's own terms
　自分の思うように
indicative of …
　…を示す

part ways
　分かれる、決別する

street-wise 世慣れた

volvement in the Korean War and, more recently, the success of Japanese automakers in the US. To add to this, the formerly white population of his neighborhood in Highland Park, a suburb of Detroit, Michigan, has recently been replaced by poor Asian families, and violent gang activity has risen at the same time. Needless to say, he is appalled when an Asian family moves in next to him. However, when he meets Sue, this begins to change.

The turning point comes after Walt saves Sue from some hoodlums and he is driving her home in his car. When Walt uses his usual offensive language on Sue as he does on everyone else, she does not get offended. Instead, she replies with her own offensive remarks. Unlike his sons, Sue communicates with Walt in a style which is very similar to his own, fighting back instead of trying to compromise. From this point on, Sue becomes an interpreter for Walt. Thanks to Sue's interpretation, he slowly begins to accept the many differences he has with his Asian neighbors and even finds similarities. The ultimate sign that he stops seeing them as "others" is when he takes Thao, the weak-willed brother of Sue, under his wing. Like Sue introduced Walt to her family's culture, Walt introduces masculinity to Thao. He teaches him to "talk like a man," helps him to get a job, and ultimately teaches him how to defend himself in the world.

Gran Torino shows that cultural barriers can be overcome if just one person takes a little time to understand the other on his/her own terms. It also shows us that barriers can be created and intensified even among families due to communication difficulties. This is a wake-up call for all of us. The next time we meet people who do or say things that seem unreasonable to us, we should postpone passing judgement until we fully understand what they intend their words or actions to mean. This could lead to finding a life-changing friend.

appalled ゾッとする

hoodlum チンピラ

take ... under one's wing …の面倒を見る

cultural barriers
文化的障壁

wake-up call 警鐘、注意
を促すもの

Comprehension Check

Read & Write

次の質問が本文の内容に合えば T（True）を、合わなければ F（False）を選びましょう。
また、その理由を本文から抜き出してみましょう。

1. Different communication styles mostly affect people of different cultures.

T / F

Why?: _____

2. Walt's dislike for Asians does not come entirely from his experience in the war.　　　　T / F

Why?: _____

3. Walt and Sue both introduce something to one another.　　　　T / F

Why?: _____

Listen & Write

🎧 DL 051~053　◎ CD1-51 ~ ◎ CD1-53

音声を聞いて空所を埋めてから、本文の内容に最も合うものを選びましょう。

1. _____ behavior _____ _____ the generation of Walt's sons and not Walt?
(A) Politeness
(B) Honesty
(C) Self-control
(D) Anger

2. _____ does Walt _____ _____ with Sue?
(A) She is a pretty girl.
(B) He saved her from hoodlums.
(C) Her brother Tao is weak.
(D) She uses rough language.

3. According to this essay, _____ can we _____ _____ with more people?
(A) Make a lot of effort to explain your opinion.
(B) Try to uncover their real thoughts.
(C) Ignore their differences.
(D) Give them time to adjust their terms.

Write & Speak

次の語句の意味を英英辞典で調べて書いてみましょう。その後で、ペアを組んで相手に説明してみましょう。

> **A:** "difference" means

> **B:** "similarity" means

🎥 Thinking about Our Diversity

次の質問について考えて、自分の意見を書いてみましょう。ペアやグループで話し合ってもかまいません。

1. Imagine that an immigrant family has moved in next door. How would you approach them? Would you try to be friendly with them? Or would you keep at a distance? What is your reason?

   _____

   _____

   _____

   _____

2. Imagine that you are an immigrant who recently moved in. How would you approach your neighbors? Would you actively try to make friends with them? Or would you avoid them? What is your reason?

   _____

   _____

   _____

   _____

Gran Torino（2008）
『グラン・トリノ』

約半世紀にわたりコンスタントに監督作を世に送り続け、『許されざる者』(92) と『ミリオンダラー・ベイビー』(04) でアカデミー賞作品賞および監督賞を受賞しているクリント・イーストウッド。本作を最後に俳優業から引退して監督に専念することを宣言したが、2018 年の『運び屋』で 88 歳にして本作以来 10 年ぶりに自身の監督作で主演を果たしている。

Column	デトロイトという街と「グラン・トリノ」という車

　『グラン・トリノ』では、クリント・イーストウッド演じるポーランド系アメリカ人で元自動車工のウォルトと隣家に引っ越してきたモン族（Hmong）一家との交流、そして一家の少年タオに対するメンター（人生の指導者）としてのウォルトの行動を中心に物語が展開する。

　モン族というのは中国の雲貴高原、ベトナム、ラオス、タイの山岳地帯に住む民族である。ベトナム戦争中、ラオスに住むモン族の多くがアメリカの情報機関である CIA に協力し、反共破壊活動をおこなった。しかし、アメリカがベトナム戦争に敗北してベトナムから撤退すると、モン族の多くは共産勢力の攻撃から逃れるためにタイに政治亡命し、さらにその一部はアメリカに移住した。映画に登場するモン族の一家もこうした政治的難民である。

　映画の舞台となっているミシガン州デトロイトは、ビッグ 3 と称される GM、フォード、クライスラーに代表される自動車産業のメッカとして、かつては全米のみならず世界一の自動車の街であり、アメリカの繁栄の象徴であった。しかし、第二次世界大戦後、失業した多くのアフリカ系アメリカ人が南部から流入を続け、67 年には人種暴動が起こった（デトロイト暴動）。この事件以降、白人は郊外に移り住むようになり、80 年には黒人人口は 63 パーセントにまで達してアメリカ最大のアフリカ系住民が暮らす都市となった。また、73 年のオイル・ショック以降の小型車ブームと日本車などの輸入車の激増によって自動車生産は大きく減少していき、失業率も急増した結果、2013 年にデトロイト市は財政破綻を表明した。ウォルトが住むハイランド・パークという住宅地も、かつては自動車産業に携わる人たちが暮らす場所であったが、自動車産業の衰退とともに白人が去っていき、犯罪が増えて荒廃した土地である。

　本作のタイトルとなっており、ウォルトが宝物のように大切にしている「グラン・トリノ」は、フォードが 1972 年から 76 年にかけて生産していた車である。いわば、アメリカの自動車産業の最後の輝きを象徴する車であり、ウォルトにとっては単なる車ではなく彼の生きてきた証しであり、生き様を象徴するものであるといえよう。なお、この車の名前はイタリアの都市トリノに由来している。トリノもまた、イタリアを代表する自動車メーカーであるフィアットの城下町として栄えた都市であり、「イタリアのデトロイト」ともいわれる。

Unit 7

An Illegal Life
"The Visitor"

The Visitor の主人公 Walter はふとしたことからシリア人の青年 Tarek と親しくなりますが、彼は不法移民でした…あなただったらどのように接しますか？

©Photo12

 Key Vocabulary Match-up   DL 054   ⊙ CD1-54

次の 1 ～ 5 の意味に合うものを a ～ e から選びましょう。

1. extension   (   )   **a.** against the law

2. flee   (   )   **b.** the status to live somewhere with official permission

3. illegal   (   )   **c.** to leave very quickly to escape danger

4. immigrant   (   )   **d.** an increase to the length, in time or size, of some-

5. residence   (   )   thing

e. a person who settles permanently in a country which is not their birth country

次の文を読みましょう。

Immigrants are individuals who have left their birth nation to live in a different one. Sometimes they are seeking a higher standard of life, sometimes they are fleeing from violence, and sometimes they have been kicked out
5 of their own country. In any case, they must work to become members of the society of that nation. However, as immigrants, their residence status is always subject to government scrutiny. Legal immigrants may have to leave suddenly if their visa is not approved for extension,
10 and people who take up residence without official documentation can be deported at any time. In either case, people who have established lives with work, friends and hobbies are sometimes forced to abandon them, affecting both that person and the people around them. *The Visitor*
15 depicts the way the very normal lives of immigrants and those around them can be torn to shreds at the whim of the government.

Tarek and his family, fleeing Syria to New York to avoid persecution due to his father's political activity, did
20 apply for official documentation. While waiting for the results, Tarek builds his life in the US, going to school and finding a girlfriend. He makes a living playing the drums, called *djembe*. Tarek is a law-abiding, normal member of US society, but there is just one law that he ends up
25 breaking. After three years, his residence application is denied: he becomes an illegal immigrant but, assured by those around him that the government does not actually care, he continues with his life. Nevertheless, his life is now illegal.

30 Lacking official documentation, Tarek has to do everything unofficially to avoid detention and possibly deportation. When legal residents rent apartments, the law protects them from fraud. Tarek, however, finds himself

residence status
居住形態
scrutiny 監視、精査

documentation
（証拠）書類、文書
deport 本国に送還する、
国外退去にする

be torn to shreds
ボロボロになる
at the whim of ...
…の気まぐれで

persecution 迫害

djembe ジャンベ（西アフ
リカ発祥の太鼓）
law-abiding 法律に従う

deportation 国外退去

renting from a suspicious man who, unknown to Tarek,
35 does not even own the apartment. Tarek and his girlfriend
make this their home but, one day, Walter, the real owner
of the apartment, comes back. Without any legal status,
Tarek has no protection and could be discovered and deported if Walter calls the police. Terrified, he has no choice
40 but to leave his new home and become homeless. Walter,
feeling for the young couple, allows them to stay with him
and the three of them become housemates.

    Walter is a widowed professor who has lost his pas-
sion for life. He discovers that Tarek is an illegal immi-
45 grant, but Tarek, whose youth and passion reignites Walter's will to live, is now an important part of his life. Then,
one normal day, Tarek is stopped by police for suspicion of
not paying the subway fee. As a result of this misunder-
standing, he is discovered for not having documentation,
50 and he is sent to a detention center with no word to anyone he knows, including Walter. When Walter finds out, he
hires a lawyer to help Tarek, but his attempts fail. Tarek
is deported and the many years he lived in the US are
lost. Meanwhile, Walter is left confused, sad, and angry at
55 the seemingly unjustified deportation by the government
of his friend.

    A nation consists of people working to support their
government and a government working to protect its people. However, when a nation is supported by the work of
60 people whom it does not protect, such as in Tarek's case,
everyone is affected. How do citizens who depend on these
troubled individuals feel when they are deported? How do
immigrants feel living under the weight that their very
existence is or could become illegal? Moreover, what does
65 it mean for them to want to live somewhere so much that
they are willing to carry that burden? Though there may
be no clear answer, *The Visitor* invites us to reconsider
what kind of people truly support a nation.

legal status 法的身分

feel for ... …に同情する
stay with ...
　…と同居する

widowed 妻を亡くした

reignite 再び火をつける、
　再燃する

detention center 拘置所

seemingly 一見すると
unjustified 不当な

Comprehension Check

Read & Write

次の質問が本文の内容に合えば T（True）を、合わなければ F（False）を選びましょう。
また、その理由を本文から抜き出してみましょう。

1. The government only deports immigrants who do not have connections in
the US.　　　　　　　　　　　　　　　　　　　　　　　　　　　　　　T / F

Why?: _____

2. There are few ways that Tarek is a bad citizen.　　　　　　　　T / F

Why?: _____

3. Nations give protection to all the people that contribute to it.　　T / F

Why?: _____

Listen & Write　　　　🎧 DL 060~062　　◎ CD1-60 ~ ◎ CD1-62

音声を聞いて空所を埋めてから、本文の内容に最も合うものを選びましょう。

1. _____ special treatment do immigrants _____ _____
the government?
(A) They are constantly watched.
(B) They have to wear armbands.
(C) They do not get residence status.
(D) They are deported.

2. _____ is most likely to happen if Tarek _____ _____
by the government?
(A) He will be taken to jail.
(B) He will have to stay in a special facility.
(C) He will have to pay a lot of money.
(D) He will have his job taken by the government.

3. _____ does Tarek _____ Walter?
(A) He gives him inspiration.
(B) He comforts him.
(C) He makes him interested in his job again.
(D) He teaches him how to sing.

Write & Speak

次の語句の意味を英英辞典で調べて書いてみましょう。その後で、ペアを組んで相手に説明してみましょう。

A: "nation" means

B: "citizen" means

🎥 Thinking about Our Diversity

次の質問について考えて、自分の意見を書いてみましょう。ペアやグループで話し合ってもかまいません。

1. Imagine that you are a legal immigrant, but your visa application has been denied. Would you continue living there anyway? Or would you give up your life there and go back to your birth country?

_____

_____

_____

_____

2. Imagine that you discover that a neighbor you were good friends with is an illegal immigrant. What sort of attitude would you take? Would you report it to the police? Or would you try to help your neighbor?

_____

_____

_____

_____

The Visitor（2007）
『扉をたたく人』

妻を亡くし単調な日々を送っていた大学教授ウォルターと、シリアからの不法移民の青年タレクとの偶然の出会いから生まれた交流を通して不法滞在の問題を描いた本作は、ウォルターを演じたリチャード・ジェンキンスが第81回アカデミー賞で主演男優賞にノミネートされた。

Column アメリカにおける移民政策の歴史

　『扉をたたく人』の舞台となっているのは2001年の9.11同時多発テロ事件以降のニューヨークである。この事件以降、アメリカは移民政策の方針を大きく変え、移民希望者や不法滞在者に対して非常に厳しい措置を取るようになった。例えば、入国時に外国人に対して従来の2倍にあたる48時間の拘束を可能にする規則が制定され、入国ビザの発給規制もおこなわれるようになった。FBIの統計によれば、テロの犯人と目されたイスラム教徒に対する2001年のヘイトクライム（人種、宗教、肌の色、民族的出自、性的指向、性別、心身の障害などを理由とした憎悪あるいは偏見を動機とする犯罪）は前年の28件から481件へと約17倍に増えたという。シリア出身のタレクが国外追放という重い処罰を受けることになった最大の原因は、彼がアラブ人でイスラム教徒であったからにほかならない。

　アメリカへの移民は17世紀に始まった。当時の移民のほとんどはイギリスなど西ヨーロッパの国々の出身者で、それ以前にアメリカで暮らしていたのはネイティブ・アメリカンと呼ばれる人々であった。1607年にはイギリス人が現在のバージニアに入植し、イギリス最初の植民地が建設された。同時期に、フランス人、オランダ人、ドイツ人、北欧の人々もアメリカに移住するようになった。

　その後、アイルランドからの移民に加え（p.35参照）、1833年にイギリスが奴隷貿易を禁止して以降はアフリカ系アメリカ人に代わる労働力として中国人の移民が増えていった。彼らは主としてカリフォルニアの金鉱開発や大陸横断鉄道建設の労働力として使役された。1890年代からは日本人移民の数も急速に増え、20世紀に入るとイタリア人、ポーランド人、ロシア人、ユダヤ人の移民が増えていった。ところが1924年の移民制限法の成立によって新しい移民は国ごとに数が制限され、日本からの移民は禁止されることになった。

　トランプ大統領は、グリーンカード（永住権）の発給を20〜60パーセント削減し、出入国管理にあたる職員を大幅に増員するという移民政策を大統領選挙の公約に掲げていたことからもわかるように、移民を抑制する政策をおこない、中南米、特にアメリカと国境を接するメキシコからの不法移民に対して強い警戒心を抱いている。前任のオバマ大統領は、入国時に15歳以下だった不法移民の若者に対して一定の条件を満たせば一時的な就労を許可したが、トランプ大統領は強制送還を免除する政策を廃止しようとしている。

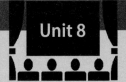

Unit 8
Foreign Language and Self-Confidence
"English Vinglish"

海外に行って言葉が通じなくて困ったり悔しい思いをしたりした経験はありませんか？ *English Vinglish* の主人公で英語が苦手なインド人主婦 Shashi のケースを見てみましょう。

©Eros International Ltd.

 Key Vocabulary Match-up　　 DL 063　　CD1-63

次の 1 ～ 5 の意味に合うものを a ～ e から選びましょう。

1. embarrassed　　(　　)

2. insult　　(　　)

3. interaction　　(　　)

4. motivation　　(　　)

5. positive　　(　　)

a. one's reason to do something

b. indicating support or approval

c. an act that hurts someone's feelings

d. feeling uncomfortable due to worries about what others think of you

e. the series of acts of responding to the behavior of others and being responded to

Reading

次の文を読みましょう。

Why do we try to learn a foreign language? Sometimes it is necessary for achieving a different goal like passing a test or getting a job, and sometimes we need it to communicate. Whatever the case, this is our "motiva-
5   tion," and our motivation is what determines what "success" means. Now, what would you do if you could not communicate when you traveled abroad? *English Vinglish* depicts how the frustration we experience in a foreign country trying to communicate in a foreign language
10 transforms into positive motivation. For the protagonist Shashi, her frustrating experience in the US gave her positive motivation to learn it, and this led to her self-confidence and success.

Shashi is a proud, wise and dutiful mother to a well-
15 off household in India, but there is one thing she often feels embarrassed about: her English. Her children use English in school to talk to their friends and teachers and her husband uses it for important meetings at work and for international clients. Shashi, however, with no real
20 need to use English, knows very little. When she does use it, her husband, her young daughter and her even younger son ridicule her for her mistakes. Since her only contact with English is the occasional insult from her family when she makes a mistake, it is understandable that she
25 has no desire to speak it.

One day, after she is forced to travel to the US by herself to attend her niece's wedding, this changes. At first, since she stays with her Hindi-speaking family there, she does fine without English. However, the situation takes a
30 turn when she goes to a local café alone and is unable to order because she cannot understand the clerk's English. Called "an idiot" and "stupid" by the clerk and customers, she flees from the café. This insult runs deeper than any

Whatever the case
いずれにせよ

dutiful 従順な
well-off 裕福な

ridicule
あざ笑う、バカにする

Hindi-speaking
ヒンディー語を話す
take a turn 変わる

before because, in the US, there is some truth to it; she
35 was not even able to order a coffee. Shashi thus finds new
motivation: the need to function in the US. She enrolls in
a 4-week English class.

Here, another change occurs. Among her classmates,
basic English is the only common language. As they grow
40 closer, they just want to communicate with one another,
not caring who has "better" or "worse" English. Shashi
stops worrying about using correct English, and instead
combines English and Hindi to get her points across. As a
result, despite her comparative lack of English skills, she
45 comes to be respected and admired by her classmates.
Shashi realizes that producing good English in itself is not
the real goal; the real goal is to get her ideas across and,
unlike her English grammar, she has great confidence in
these. With new confidence from this realization, her abili-
50 ty to communicate in English skyrockets. She makes successful orders at cafés and even makes a speech at her
niece's wedding that touches the hearts of all the attendees.
Confidence made Shashi into a great speaker of English.

When we begin learning a foreign language in school,
55 we are expected to strive for a certain "level," aiming to
eventually become like native speakers. This situation
sets us up to always feel inadequate no matter how much
we learn because a native speaker, by definition, is always "better." Many people who live abroad become fluent
60 not because they learn a lot of grammar or vocabulary but
because they are immersed in the culture and come to
have many successful interactions with others in that
language. They realize that if they succeed in communi-
cating with others, whether they are native speakers of
65 the language or not, their words are just as valuable as
those of anyone else. Language is not a tool for self-appraisal but for sharing our thoughts with others. Devel-
oping the confidence to do that is the key to "success" in
learning a foreign language.

enroll in ... …に登録する

get across ...
　…を理解させる、…をわ
　からせる
comparative 相対的な

skyrocket
　飛躍的に上昇する

attendee 出席者

strive for ...
　…に向かって努力する

by definition
　定義上、当然のこととし
　て

be immersed in ...
　…にどっぷり浸かる

self-appraisal
　自己評価

Comprehension Check

Read & Write

次の質問が本文の内容に合えば T（True）を、合わなければ F（False）を選びましょう。
また、その理由を本文から抜き出してみましょう。

1. Shashi felt the need to learn English before going to the US.　　　T / F

Why?: _____

2. Shashi's classmates look up to her even though she has poor English.　T / F

Why?: _____

3. Language is a good way to measure one's worth.　　　　　　　T / F

Why?: _____

Listen & Write

DL 069~071　CD1-69 ~ CD1-71

音声を聞いて空所を埋めてから、本文の内容に最も合うものを選びましょう。

1. _____ isn't Shashi _____ _____ learning English at first?

(A) She often ridicules her children.

(B) It is too difficult.

(C) She only needs it with her children.

(D) Her family makes fun of her.

2. _____ do Shashi and her classmates _____ _____ each other in English?

(A) They speak it well.

(B) The teacher makes them.

(C) They do not share any other languages.

(D) They like it a lot.

3. _____ is the reason that many people who _____ _____ become fluent in a foreign language?

(A) Grammar skills

(B) Vocabulary knowledge

(C) Talking to others often

(D) Intelligence

Write & Speak

次の語句の意味を英英辞典で調べて書いてみましょう。その後で、ペアを組んで相手に説明してみましょう。

A: "communicate" means

B: "confidence" means

Thinking about Our Diversity

次の質問について考えて、自分の意見を書いてみましょう。ペアやグループで話し合ってもかまいません。

1. Imagine that you have gone to a café in another country and you do not know how to order. What would you do to get your order across to the clerk?

_____

_____

_____

_____

2. Imagine that you are in line at a café and that you are in a hurry. However, there is a foreign visitor in front of you who does not know how to order. How would you react?

_____

_____

_____

_____

English Vinglish（2012）
『マダム・イン・ニューヨーク』

派手なダンスやアクションのいわゆる「ボリウッド映画」のイメージを変え、笑いと感動をもたらす本作。主人公のシャシを演じたシュリデヴィ（Sridevi）はインドの国民的女優で、本作で15年ぶりに復帰した。

ブルーレイ＆DVD発売中
ブルーレイ 4,300円（税抜）／DVD 3,800円（税抜）
発売・販売元：アミューズソフト

インドと英語の関係

　映画の冒頭、主人公のシャシは英字新聞とヒンディー語の新聞から後者を選んで読み始める。この場面はインドでの使用言語を象徴している。現在のインドの公用語はヒンディー語であるが、長年にわたって英語による教育がおこなわれてきたため、英語が準公用語となっている。その原因はインドとイギリスとの長い関係による。

　インドとイギリスの本格的な関係は1600年のイギリス東インド会社（East Indian Company）の設立から始まる。その主な目的は、インドで栽培された綿花から作られた綿織物をイギリスに輸入することにあった。1757年、インドに進出してきたフランス東インド会社との戦いに勝利したイギリス東インド会社は、インドでの覇権を確立したことで単なる貿易商社から植民地支配機関へと転換を遂げた。1835年からは英語で教育がおこなわれ、官庁の文書はすべて英語で作成することが義務付けられた結果、英語が急速に普及することとなった。インド以外で英語を公用語にしているアジアの国には、同じくイギリスの植民地であったシンガポール、パキスタン、香港、アメリカの植民地であったフィリピンなどがある。

　インドではIndian EnglishまたはHinglish（Hindi + English）と呼ばれる発音・語彙・文法においてヒンディー語の影響を受けた英語を話す人も多い。ただし、2005年に実施されたインド人間開発調査での英語力についての質問では、「英語で流暢に会話ができる」と答えた人はわずか4パーセント、「少しできる」と答えた人も14パーセントにすぎない。英語力には学歴によって大きな違いがみられ、大卒以上の学歴を持つ人の9割近くが英語を話せると答えたのに対して、中等教育卒の人では5割程度、初等教育卒の人では1割強しかいない。学歴による差がこれほど大きい原因のひとつとして、世界第2位の13億2400万人という人口のうち、2010年代になっても高等教育機関に進学する人の割合が2割程度と少数であることが挙げられる。本作の主人公シャシも初等教育しか受けておらず、夫は大卒で、娘は中等教育の段階ではあるが英語で授業がおこなわれる学校に通っており、英語でのコミュニケーションに苦労していないところからも、このような国内事情が見て取れるだろう。

　なお、原題 English Vinglish のVinglishは特に意味はなく、インドではこのように似た音の言葉を並べてリズム感を出して遊ぶことがあるとのことである。

Unit 9

— **Cross-Cultural Communication**

Frame of Mind

"Lost in Translation"

インバウンド市場の拡大に伴い、日本を訪れる外国人観光客の数は増加の一途をたどっています。彼らの目に日本や日本人の姿はどのように映っているのでしょうか。*Lost in Translation* の主人公 Bob のケースを見てみましょう。

©Collection Christophel

 Key Vocabulary Match-up　 DL 072　CD2-02

次の１～５の意味に合うものをa～eから選びましょう。

1. attitude　　　（　）
2. impression　　（　）
3. instruction　　（　）
4. translation　　（　）
5. treatment　　 （　）

a. a statement telling someone how to behave

b. a way of behaving in response to something

c. the process of changing something into a corresponding form

d. a way of thinking about something that influences how you act toward it

e. a judgment you form of something based on one or more encounters with it

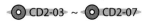
次の文を読みましょう。

You are a confident professional who has come to a foreign country temporarily to do your job. However, no one around you understands what you are saying, nor do you understand what they are saying. Your confidence be-
5　gins to fade. Everyone but you seems to understand how things work, making you feel constantly inadequate. You are always on guard, and all you want is to go home. This unpleasant experience is common to people who face new foreign cultures alone. It seems like "us" against "them"
10　and each difference seems like a challenge to our personal sensibilities. *Lost in Translation* shows us how Bob, an American actor in Japan for work, overcomes this initial sense of hostility and leaves Japan with a very positive impression.

15　Bob has been hired to represent a Japanese whiskey brand in Japan. Although he is given first-class treat-ment, Japan presents him with countless challenges to his sense of adequacy as an actor, and even as a function-al adult. The most representative example is at a com-
20　mercial shoot. A Japanese interpreter is present because the director does not speak English, but her English translations are crude, to say the least. Although Bob tries to guess the director's instructions based on his act-ing experience, he largely fails, and the director gets in-
25　creasingly frustrated because Bob's acting is not reflect-ing his instructions. As a seasoned actor, this is a humiliating experience for Bob.

After this, countless small differences accumulate, alienating Bob more and more. The shower head in his
30　luxurious hotel room is below his head, he injures himself in the hotel gym because he cannot understand the ver-bal instructions on a treadmill, he cannot even oblige a call girl sent to him by his client because he cannot un-

on guard
警戒して、用心して

hostility 敵意

adequacy
適切であること
functional adult
まともな大人

to say the least
控えめに言っても

seasoned 経験豊富な、
ベテランの
humiliating 屈辱的な

luxurious 豪華な

treadmill トレッドミル、
ランニングマシン
oblige 願いをかなえる

derstand her English, thinking she is asking him to "lip"
35 her stockings instead of "rip" them. Understandably,
when there is a request for him to appear on a highly
popular Japanese talk show, he refuses it, wanting to escape as soon as possible and return to being a competent
professional.

40   However, a change in his attitude comes after he
spends a night out with Charlotte, a young American
woman, and her Japanese friends. When they go to karaoke, he finds himself enjoying the foreign culture for the
first time. After this, Charlotte and Bob start to share
45 their funny experiences in Japan: Japanese people switch-
ing their *r*'s and *l*'s in English, not being able to eat prop-
erly at a sushi restaurant, not being able to get around
due to a lack of street signs, etc. Their common struggle to
get by in Japan reduces Bob's feeling of inadequacy, and
50 he begins to enjoy the differences instead of viewing them
as threats. At one point, Bob even calls his wife to tell her
about how fun Japan is and that he wants to adopt a
healthy Japanese-like diet. In fact, Bob even changes his
mind about the talk show; he decides that he wants to
55 stay in Japan a little longer. At the TV show, he, as usual,
has no idea what people are saying, but he enjoys himself
nonetheless. When he finally leaves Japan, he does so
with a very positive impression of the new culture.

      Like many, Bob found it difficult to remain objective
60 at first. However, he found a solution by finding a
like-minded American friend to share his experiences
with. When we have to get by in foreign cultures, whether
it be for work like Bob or for study like many college students, the foreign culture can seem hostile because it
65 seems like we are the only ones who are different. However, this sensation of being challenged is usually just a
frame of mind. Like Bob, we should change our frame of
mind to recognize cultural differences and language barriers as opportunities for exploration and learning.

get around 動き回る

get by 何とかやっていく

Japanese-like diet
日本的な食生活

as usual いつものように

like-minded
同じ考えをもつ、気の合
う

frame of mind
心構え、気の持ちよう

Comprehension Check

Read & Write

次の質問が本文の内容に合えば T （True）を、合わなければ F （False）を選びましょう。
また、その理由を本文から抜き出してみましょう。

1. Living in a foreign culture can feel like a fight. T / F

Why?: _____

2. Bob learns to like Japan by ignoring the differences from his culture. T / F

Why?: _____

3. It takes effort to see foreign cultures as ways to learn new things. T / F

Why?: _____

Listen & Write

DL 078~080 · CD2-08 ~ CD2-10

音声を聞いて空所を埋めてから、本文の内容に最も合うものを選びましょう。

1. _____ is Bob _____ in Japan?
   (A) Like a low-class person
   (B) Like someone who cannot do their job
   (C) Like an alien
   (D) Like a competent adult

2. _____ _____ about a change in Bob's _____ of mind?
   (A) A new friend
   (B) A shocking experience
   (C) An experience of eating incorrectly
   (D) A chance to sing karaoke

3. _____ does Bob _____ Japan when he leaves?
   (A) It is a frustrating place.
   (B) It is an interesting place.
   (C) The diet there is very healthy.
   (D) He would rather not visit again.

Write & Speak

次の語句の意味を英英辞典で調べて書いてみましょう。その後で、ペアを組んで相手に説明してみましょう。

> **A:** "challenge" means

> **B:** "hostile" means

🎥 Thinking about Our Diversity

次の質問について考えて、自分の意見を書いてみましょう。ペアやグループで話し合ってもかまいません。

1. Imagine that you are staying abroad for a period of time, but you feel isolated because you are having trouble blending in. Would you decide you do not like that country, or would you try to find good points? How might you go about finding good points?

   _____

   _____

   _____

   _____

2. What could you do to make a foreign visitor who is having trouble understanding Japan feel welcome? Where would you take them? What else could you do for them?

   _____

   _____

   _____

   _____

Lost in Translation（2003）
『ロスト・イン・トランスレーション』

日本に滞在中の2人のアメリカ人が異国で感じる孤独や戸惑いを通して自分自身と向き合う姿を描いたソフィア・コッポラ監督による本作。第76回アカデミー賞では作品賞・監督賞・主演男優賞など4部門にノミネートされ、脚本賞を受賞した。

Column 「ローコンテクスト文化」と「ハイコンテクスト文化」

　アメリカの文化人類学者エドワード・T・ホールは、言語によるコミュニケーションのあり方を説明するための用語として、「ローコンテクスト文化」（low-context cultures：低文脈文化）と「ハイコンテクスト文化」（high-context cultures：高文脈文化）を提唱した。ここでいう「コンテクスト＝文脈」とは、相手と共通して持っている知識や価値観のことである。そうしたものが少なく、言語に依存して意思伝達がおこなわれる傾向が強い文化が「ローコンテクスト文化」である。一般的に欧米の国々は「ローコンテクスト文化」が支配的で、言葉によるコミュニケーションが重要視される。それに対して「ハイコンテクスト文化」では、いわゆる「以心伝心」で意思の疎通がおこなわれる傾向が強い。「空気を読む」ことや「忖度」することが重要視される日本は「ハイコンテクスト文化」の強い国であるといえるであろう。

　本作では、この「ローコンテクスト文化」と「ハイコンテクスト文化」の軋轢が見られる。ウイスキーのCM撮影のために初めて日本を訪れた初老のハリウッドスターであるボブは、撮影現場でディレクターにいろいろ注文を付けられる。ところが、通訳はディレクターの言葉を正確には伝えず、大幅にカットして訳す。ボブはディレクターが何を言っているのかまったく理解できないが、明らかに話している言葉の分量が違うことから通訳が一部しか訳していないことに気づいており、"Is that everything? It seemed like he said quite a bit more than that." と言う。ボブは言語によるコミュニケーションが主体となるアメリカ人なので、訳出されていない文に対して非常に神経質になっていることがわかるであろう。また、同じホテルに宿泊しているシャーロットという若いアメリカ人女性としゃぶしゃぶを食べに行き、メニューを見てもどれも同じ肉に見え、自分で料理をしなければならないとは最悪だと語り合う場面がある。この場合も、2つの文化の間の離隔から生じるコミュニケーション不全を示している。

　この映画では音楽がクローズアップされていることも見逃してはならない。言語を媒体としない場合、音楽は「ローコンテクスト文化」と「ハイコンテクスト文化」を架橋するものである。ボブとシャーロットが日本人とカラオケに興じている場面は、そのことを象徴しているといえよう。

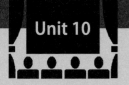

Unit 10

— **State Welfare**

An Individual or A Number

"I, Daniel Blake"

誰もが病気になったり年老いたりして仕事ができなくなる可能性があります。また、急に仕事を失うことも
あります。そのような場合、国はどのくらい親身になって助けてくれるでしょうか。I, Daniel Blake では社
会保障制度に翻弄される人々の姿が描かれています。

©Collection Christophel

 Key Vocabulary Match-up 🎧 DL 081 💿 CD2-11

次の 1 ～ 5 の意味に合うものを a ～ e から選びましょう。

1. benefits	( )	**a.** having no job
2. complex	( )	**b.** repeating the same pattern
3. mechanical	( )	**c.** made of many interacting parts
4. moral	( )	**d.** money intended to help a certain group of people who need financial help
5. unemployed	( )	**e.** relating to whether some act agrees with a set of social values

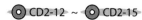
次の文を読みましょう。

Any large society will include honest, hard-working individuals who, due to difficult circumstances, need financial support to survive: those who were suddenly unemployed, those with a medical condition, the handi-
5 capped, single mothers, etc. State welfare is intended to help these individuals, but it is a large, complicated and inflexible system, much like a machine. Further complicating matters, each person's case is unique so, for many, finding a way to fit into the machine's program is a great
10 struggle. Making it even worse, there is a general tendency to look down on them as lazy individuals trying to get money without working for it. *I, Daniel Blake* portrays how even honest people struggle before the complex machine called state welfare and how the presence or the
15 lack of moral support from other people affects their struggle.

Protagonist Daniel Blake, now almost 60, was a carpenter for his whole life, but when he contracts a heart ailment, to his disappointment, his doctor forbids him
20 from working. He decides he has no choice but to apply for welfare, but the state's point system deems him 2 points short of unfitness to work, leaving him not only unable to work but ineligible for welfare. He applies for an appeal, but until it is processed his only choice to find a way to
25 pay the bills is to apply for a different welfare program, job-seekers' support. To qualify for this, he has to search for a job even though medically he cannot take one. In fact, he succeeds in getting work but has to refuse his employer, who then asks him, "So you prefer to be on ben-
30 efits than do a day's graft?" This does the opposite of moral support, smashing Daniel's pride. He ends up giving up his struggle for benefits, even knowing that he may not survive without them.

inflexible 柔軟性のない、融通の利かない

ailment 病気

unfitness 不能

ineligible 資格がない

graft 労働

What restored Daniel's will to fight was the moral
35 support of Daisy and her mother, Katie. Katie is a likewise-troubled single mother he had helped throughout
the movie by looking after her children, especially Daisy.
After he has given up, Daisy comes to him and, although
he tries to turn her away, she manages to appeal to his
40 sensibilities with her simple, innocent childhood logic.

"Can I ask you one question, Dan? Did you help us?"

"Suppose so."

"So why can't I help you?"

Accepting her help does not change the misfortune of his
45 situation, but he realizes there are people that care about
him as an individual, that he is not just a number in a
machine or a lazy man trying to get money for nothing.
He resumes his struggle to win support.

Daniel's story shows us the unreasonable demands
50 state welfare systems can put on a person, and how the
humans who are employed to run this machine can be
equally mechanical, pushing people through the system
without a thought for their situations. Until society can
come up with a better system, this is a truth we must deal
55 with. However, for people in this struggle, each instance
of human warmth and respect can help them keep going
while each instance of disrespect from others contributes
to killing them. We should avoid the general tendency to
judge those seeking welfare as insincere and lazy with
60 little idea of what their circumstances are. Instead, we
can offer them our warm support in rebuilding their lives.
After all, just like Katie and her daughter did for Daniel,
the individuals we help might just come around and do
the same for us when we are in trouble.

likewise-troubled
同じように問題を抱えた

insincere 不誠実な

Comprehension Check

Read & Write

次の質問が本文の内容に合えば T（True）を、合わなければ F（False）を選びましょう。
また、その理由を本文から抜き出してみましょう。

1. State welfare is a robotic system which hurts people in trouble.　　　T / F

Why?: _____

2. People often have a poor opinion of those who receive state welfare.　　T / F

Why?: _____

3. State welfare systems always get some humanity from the humans who run
them.　　　　　　　　　　　　　　　　　　　　　　　　　　　　T / F

Why?: _____

Listen & Write

🎧 DL 086~088　　⊙ CD2-16 ～ ⊙ CD2-18

音声を聞いて空所を埋めてから、本文の内容に最も合うものを選びましょう。

1. _____ do many people fail to _____ _____ from state
welfare?
(A) They are unusual.
(B) They have broken the law.
(C) They cannot fill out the forms.
(D) They are too normal.

2. _____ does Daniel decide to _____ _____ a job again?
(A) He wants to work.
(B) The doctor told him to.
(C) It is necessary to get government support.
(D) He felt that he had to morally.

3. _____ is the biggest reason for Daniel _____ _____ on
getting help?
(A) The frustrating paperwork
(B) Unkind clerks
(C) Impossible decisions
(D) A lack of encouragement from others

Write & Speak

次の語句の意味を英英辞典で調べて書いてみましょう。その後で、ペアを組んで相手に説明してみましょう。

A: "welfare" means

B: "support" means

Thinking about Our Diversity

次の質問について考えて、自分の意見を書いてみましょう。ペアやグループで話し合ってもかまいません。

1. Imagine that you have fallen ill and can no longer work. You went to the state welfare office and were told that you do not qualify for benefits. What would you do?

_____

_____

_____

_____

2. You are an employee of the state welfare office. An elderly person who can no longer work due to illness has come to apply for welfare, but they do not qualify. What would you do?

_____

_____

_____

_____

I, Daniel Blake（2016）
『わたしは、ダニエル・ブレイク』

労働者階級や移民など社会的弱者を描き続けてきたイギリスを代表する映画監督であるケン・ローチ。イギリスのみならず世界中に拡大する格差や貧困を伝えるために引退を撤回して制作した本作は、第69回カンヌ国際映画祭で『麦の穂をゆらす風』（06）に続いて自身2度目となるパルム・ドール（最高賞）を受賞した。

Column イギリスの過酷な社会保障制度

　『わたしは、ダニエル・ブレイク』はイギリスの厳しい社会保障制度を背景とした作品である。イギリスの社会派監督として知られるケン・ローチ（1936-　）は本作で、仕事中に心臓発作に見舞われて医師から仕事を止められた59歳の大工ダニエル・ブレイクと、ロンドンのホームレス保護施設から引っ越してきた2人の子どもを抱えるシングルマザーのケイティが直面する社会的弱者いじめともいうべき現今の過酷な社会保障制度を告発している。"My name is Daniel Blake, I am a man, not a dog" と自己の尊厳を訴えるダニエルの魂の叫びともいうべき言葉からも推察しえるように、この映画では現在の社会保障制度が人間の尊厳さえも踏みにじるものであることを訴えている。公開当時、イギリスの労働党党首ジェレミー・コービンは国会で本作に言及し、メイ首相に対して見ることを勧めたとのことである。

　第二次世界大戦後、イギリスは戦後社会の復興の柱として「ゆりかごから墓場まで」（from the cradle to the grave）をスローガンとする社会保障制度の充実に取り組んだ。イギリスの社会保障制度は先進国のモデルとなったが、1960 ～ 70年代に経済成長が長期的に停滞したため（俗に The British disease「イギリス病」と呼ばれる）、80年代に入るとマーガレット・サッチャー首相によって、政府の財政を圧迫していると考えられた社会保障費が削減されることになった。90年代前半にサッチャーの後を継いで首相となった保守党のジョン・メージャーも福祉削減を踏襲した。97年に首相となった労働党のトニー・ブレアは福祉政策を重視し、新しい福祉国家を実現しようと試みたが成功しなかった。その後、2007年に首相となった労働党のゴードン・ブラウンも有効な福祉政策を打ち出すことができなかった。2010年に首相となった保守党のデービッド・キャメロンはサッチャー以上の厳しい社会保障制度改革を実行した。その結果、福祉と住宅手当および社会保障の削減が重なったために、2010年以降、障害者は健常者と比べて9倍、重度障害者に至っては19倍もの厳しい生活を強いられるようになったといわれる。障害の認定に関しては、「片手に指が一本でもあれば就労可能」と皮肉られるほど非常に厳しい。2016年5月12日付のデイリー・ミラー紙は、頭蓋骨の半分を失って重度の記憶障害と半身麻痺を患う男性に対して、労働年金省が「就労可能」との裁定を下したことを伝えている。

Unit 11
Pushing Past Boundaries
"The Theory of Everything"

ある日突然、自分の身体が自由に動かなくなったとしたら？　また、あなたの身のまわりの人がもしそのようになったら？　イギリスの理論物理学者 Stephen Hawking と彼を支えたパートナー Jane の実話をもとにした *The Theory of Everything* のケースを見てみましょう。

©Collection Christophel

Key Vocabulary Match-up　 DL 089　◎ CD2-19

次の１～５の意味に合うものを a ～ e から選びましょう。

1. disease　　　　（　）
2. physical　　　　（　）
3. physics　　　　（　）
4. restriction　　　（　）
5. voluntary　　　 （　）

a. done based on one's own will
b. a limit on the possibilities of something
c. related to aspects of the body other than the mind
d. the study of the relationship between matter and energy
e. a harmful condition which can affect any living thing

次の文を読みましょう。

In our lives, we all want to find a significant way to contribute to the world. Of course, to do so we often have to challenge our own boundaries. For example, students cannot succeed at a foreign university unless they learn the local language, but once they do, they may easily surpass the native-speaking students in academic performance. A person without money cannot start a business, but if they convince people to invest, the business they create may enjoy great success. Physical disabilities also set boundaries, but these boundaries are often regarded as permanent. This results in physically handicapped individuals being viewed as having little merit for society. *The Theory of Everything* refutes this, showing that, with enough support, physically handicapped individuals can push past their boundaries and change the world.

Stephen Hawking is witty, has many good friends, attends a prestigious university and has a profound gift for physics. Unfortunately, he contracts ALS, a severely disabling disease. ALS results in the loss of all voluntary muscle movement, erasing the ability to speak, eat, move and even breathe. His doctor, his family, his friends and he himself are all convinced that writing out physics formulas, reading books, discussing his ideas with others, and even relieving himself would all become inaccessible to him. Rather than encourage him to fight his limits, they band together in resignation, giving up any hope for his future.

His savior was his girlfriend Jane. After he has given up hope, she forces him to play a game of croquet with her. As she sees him stumble and fall, she realizes how disabled he is. However, unlike the rest of his friends and family, instead of pitying him, she pledges to fight the disease with him until the end. Stephen, knowing that she saw his disability and was still willing to fight with him,

academic performance
学業成績

refute
論破する、反証する

ALS 筋萎縮性側索硬化症
(Amyotrophic Lateral Sclerosis)

relieve oneself 用を足す

savior 救い主

croquet クロッケー
（イギリス発祥の芝生の
上でボールを打つ球技）

gains hope. Stephen confronts increasing restrictions on
35 his physical abilities, but thanks to Jane's support, he
maintains his focus and finds great success with physics.
He gets an electronic wheel chair for mobility, allowing
him to teach classes and give university lectures. He gets
an automatic synthesizer so he can talk and communi-
40 cate, allowing him to write a book which wins a prestigious award. His research becomes renowned throughout
the world.

All the while, there are many things he cannot do. He
cannot run around with his children, go camping, or talk
45 and communicate normally. Jane's love and support for
him despite his shortcomings is essential to his success.
However, this comes at the cost of Jane's own ambitions.
She has to give up her own ambitions and dreams, and
eventually reaches her emotional limit. Stephen and Jane
50 separate. Indeed, with the help of those around him, Stephen not only lives to an old age, completely violating the
2-year prognosis given to him by the doctor when he was
diagnosed, but revolutionizes our understanding of the
universe. However, the strain on Jane shows that society
55 does not yet provide enough support for handicapped people, no matter how talented they are, to be self-sufficient.

The Theory of Everything shows us that while there
are many things people with physical disability cannot
do, there are many things they can. Indeed, Stephen
60 achieved things no one else could achieve. Nevertheless, if
by chance he had never met Jane or she had been a little
less determined to help him, his amazing contribution to
physics would have been impossible. We can only wonder
how many amazing discoveries we have lost throughout
65 history due to physical disability. Giving proof that helping the physically handicapped to get past their boundaries can change the world, Stephen and Jane's story gives
strong motivation for us to act as a society to support the
disabled rather than leave it up to individuals.

synthesizer
シンセサイザー

shortcoming 短所、欠点

at the cost of ...
　…を犠牲にして

prognosis 予後

self-sufficient 自分のこ
　とは自分でできる

by chance
　偶然、たまたま

Comprehension Check

Read & Write

次の質問が本文の内容に合えば T（True）を、合わなければ F（False）を選びましょう。
また、その理由を本文から抜き出してみましょう。

1. Physical disabilities are never regarded as permanent. 　　　　T / F

Why?: _____

2. Jane's support helps Stephen reduce his physical disability. 　　T / F

Why?: _____

3. Dedicating herself to supporting Stephen made Jane completely satisfied.

T / F

Why?: _____

Listen & Write

🎧 DL 095~097　　◎ CD2-25 ~ ◎ CD2-27

音声を聞いて空所を埋めてから、本文の内容に最も合うものを選びましょう。

1. _____ do Stephen's friends and family _____ _____
his condition?
(A) They distance themselves from him.
(B) They encourage him to accept his fate.
(C) They stop loving him.
(D) They decide to fight for his future.

2. _____ did Jane _____ _____ giving Stephen hope?
(A) She recognized his true state and still believed in him.
(B) She was able to look past his condition.
(C) She convinced him that his sickness could be cured.
(D) She loved him more than his family.

3. _____ suggests that we do not give _____ _____ to
the handicapped?
(A) Jane's emotions
(B) Stephen's struggle
(C) Stephen and Jane's separation
(D) Jane's incredible support

Write & Speak

次の語句の意味を英英辞典で調べて書いてみましょう。その後で、ペアを組んで相手に説明してみましょう。

A: "boundary" means

B: "disability" means

🎥 Thinking about Our Diversity

次の質問について考えて、自分の意見を書いてみましょう。ペアやグループで話し合ってもかまいません。

1. Imagine that you have suddenly lost control of your body and cannot continue your current lifestyle. How would you feel? How would you face reality?

_____

_____

_____

_____

2. Imagine that one of your family members has suddenly lost the ability to control their body and cannot continue their current lifestyle. How would you support them? What kind of support do you think society should provide?

_____

_____

_____

_____

The Theory of Everything（2014）
『博士と彼女のセオリー』

イギリスの理論物理学者スティーヴン・ホーキングと妻ジェーンとの半生を描いた本作は、第87回アカデミー賞で作品賞・主演男優賞・主演女優賞など5部門にノミネートされ、ホーキングを演じたエディ・レッドメインが主演男優賞を受賞した。

Column　ALS（筋萎縮性側索硬化症）と2人のスター

ALS（Amyotrophic Lateral Sclerosis：筋萎縮性側索硬化症）は、身体を動かす際に用いられる「運動ニューロン」（motor neuron）という神経が障害を受け、運動や呼吸に必要な筋肉が徐々に衰えていく疾患である。この難病が広く知られるようになったのは、本作の主人公である相対性理論と量子力学を結合させた「車椅子の天才物理学者」スティーヴン・ホーキング博士（1942-2018）の活躍に負うところが大きい。

　ホーキングよりも前に、ALSに罹患しながらアメリカのメジャーリーグベースボール（MLB）に不朽の名を残したスーパースターがいる。この映画でホーキングが学友に自分の病名を説明する際に言及しているルー・ゲーリック（1903-41）である（ALSはゲーリックの名前を取ってLou Gehrig's diseaseとも称される）。ゲーリックはベーブ・ルース（1895-1948）とともにニューヨーク・ヤンキースの第1期黄金時代を担った大打者で、歴代最高の一塁手とされている。彼は1925年から39年

までの14年間、当時の世界記録となる2130試合連続出場を果たした。この記録は87年に広島東洋カープの衣笠祥雄に更新されるまで47年間に渡り世界記録でありつづけた。衣笠の2215試合連続出場の記録は、96年にボルチモア・オリオールズのカル・リプケンに更新されたが、「鉄の馬」と呼ばれたゲーリックがALSのために連続出場を断念することがなければ、リプケンの持つ2632試合連続出場の記録を上回っていたかもしれない。

　2017年現在、日本には約1万人のALS患者がいる。年齢層は中年以降が多く、最も多いのが60～70代である。非常に稀ではあるが、ホーキングのように若い年代で発症することもある。ALSの原因は明らかになっていないが、約10パーセントが遺伝によるもので、残りの90パーセントは遺伝の関与なしに発症している。初期症状は手に現れることが多く、患者によっては口や足に症状が現れることもある。進行すると徐々に自分の意志で身体を動かすことが難しくなり、歩行が困難になっていく。さらに進行すると、自分で呼吸することができなくなり、人工呼吸器が必要になる。また、運動ニューロンのみが阻害されるため意識ははっきりしており、精神的な働きはまったく阻害されないことも大きな特徴である（以上のALSの説明は、一部の文言を変えてmedicalnote.jpのALSからの引用）。

Unit 12
Does It Divide or Unite?
"Dallas Buyers Club"

まったく予期せず HIV に感染していると診断され、余命 1 カ月と宣告されたらあなたはどうしますか？
Dallas Buyers Club の主人公 Ron Woodroof の現実にあったケースを見てみましょう。

©Photo12

 ## Key Vocabulary Match-up　　　 🎧 DL 098　◉ CD2-28

次の 1 〜 5 の意味に合うものを a 〜 e から選びましょう。

1. comfort　　　　（　）　　**a.** the process of returning to a state of good health
2. empathy　　　　（　）　　**b.** the need for immediate action
3. indifferent　　（　）　　**c.** a state of being relaxed or satisfied
4. recovery　　　（　）　　**d.** not caring about someone or something
5. urgency　　　　（　）　　**e.** the ability to understand how others feel

次の文を読みましょう。

No human is the same, but neither are they entirely different. At any time, former enemies can become new allies and vice versa. Depending on our dominant perspective at the time, our sense of community can collapse,
5 and a new one can form. For example, for the terminally ill, their sense of urgency regarding their life gives them a deep empathy for one another, which those without such a condition could never understand. Ron Woodroof, protagonist of *Dallas Buyers Club*, is one such individual.
10 Struck with a 30-day prognosis after being diagnosed HIV Positive, his old community collapses entirely and he forms a new one which had been unthinkable for him before.

Ron, homophobic and a womanizer, cannot believe it
15 when he is diagnosed with HIV. To Ron and the majority of people in the 80s, HIV and AIDS were for homosexuals only. It is only after he discovers that it can also be caught through heterosexual sex that he accepts the diagnosis and comes to terms with his mortality. His friends offer
20 not comfort and support but scorn, vandalizing his property and calling him a faggot. The medical system in the US seems equally indifferent to Ron's shortened lifespan, preventing him from obtaining life-prolonging medicine due to having not gone through all the proper procedures.
25 Although Ron's time is limited, the government has all the time it wants.

Carrying a sense of urgency that no one around him can comprehend, Ron attends a support meeting for HIV patients looking for answers. However, when an effemi-
30 nate male tries to welcome him, Ron greets him with threats and quickly leaves. For him, there can be no "community" including both him and homosexuals. He determines to help himself and goes on a journey to Mexico to

vice versa
逆もまた同じ
sense of community
共同体意識、連帯感
the terminally ill
末期患者

homophobic
同性愛嫌悪の
womanizer 女たらし

heterosexual 異性愛の

come to terms with …
…を受け入れる、…と折
り合いをつける
mortality 死すべき運命
scorn 軽蔑、冷笑
vandalize 破壊する

life-prolonging 延命の

get AIDS medicine. There, thanks to the doctor's lifestyle
35 advice and a cocktail of drugs and vitamins that are not
legally available in the US, he makes a miraculous recovery. Ron discovers that he can to some extent extend his
life if he makes the right lifestyle changes.

When Ron returns to the states, he changes his life
40 around. However, he needs more than a way to extend his
life to feel content: he needs to feel he is accomplishing
something worthwhile in his limited time. At one point,
he confesses, "Sometimes I just feel like I'm fighting for a
life I just ain't got time to live. I want it to mean some-
45 thing." Where he finds meaning is where he would have
least expected it.

To make a living, Ron creates the Dallas Buyers Club
and partners with a transsexual woman named Rayon.
They sell the medicine he smuggled from Mexico to Amer-
50 ican AIDS patients, who are mostly homosexuals. His
work to keep the Dallas Buyers Club afloat despite inter-
ference from the government inspires its members to help
him, providing money, shelter and moral support. He discovers a community in these people who share his sense
55 of urgency in life, discovering a greater kinship with them
than he had ever felt for his former friends. Through this
community, Ron finds meaning in his life by helping individuals suffering from the same disease as him to take
control of their lives.

60 Sexuality, race, religion, culture, disease—all of these
things can divide us, but they can unite us just as well.
Ron, abandoned by his friends and even his government
due to his condition and diverging values, found purpose
in life and a powerful sense of community thanks to the
65 very same condition. When you let go of one way of seeing
the world, you can gain an entirely new one.

miraculous 奇跡的な

to some extent ある程度

transsexual 性転換の

smuggle 密輸する

keep ... afloat …を破綻
  させないようにする

kinship 親近感

take control of ...
  …を管理する

diverging 異なる

let go of ... …を手放す、
  …を取り除く

Comprehension Check

Read & Write

次の質問が本文の内容に合えば T（True）を、合わなければ F（False）を選びましょう。
また、その理由を本文から抜き出してみましょう。

1. Most people in the 80s believed that HIV/AIDS was a disease for sexually
active people and homosexuals.　　　　　　　　　　　　　　　　T / F

　　Why?: _____

2. Ron attends a meeting for HIV patients because his friends do not
understand his situation.　　　　　　　　　　　　　　　　　　　T / F

　　Why?: _____

3. Ron is not satisfied with having a longer life.　　　　　　　　　T / F

　　Why?: _____

Listen & Write　　　　　　　　🎧 DL 105~107　💿 CD2-35 ~ 💿 CD2-37

音声を聞いて空所を埋めてから、本文の内容に最も合うものを選びましょう。

1. _____ does Ron have to _____ _____ Mexico?
　　(A) The American government is too slow.
　　(B) He wanted to escape his hometown.
　　(C) His American friends forced him to leave.
　　(D) He went there to get cheaper AIDS medicine.

2. _____ made Ron _____ a new _____ with his former
enemies?
　　(A) They were homosexual.
　　(B) They were concerned with their lifespans.
　　(C) He felt morally responsible.
　　(D) No one else would accept him.

3. _____ best describes Ron's _____ in life?
　　(A) Saving the terminally ill
　　(B) Helping people like him
　　(C) Fighting for gay rights
　　(D) Finding a cure for AIDS

Write & Speak

次の語句の意味を英英辞典で調べて書いてみましょう。その後で、ペアを組んで相手に説明してみましょう。

A: "community" means

B: "sexuality" means

🎥 Thinking about Our Diversity

次の質問について考えて、自分の意見を書いてみましょう。ペアやグループで話し合ってもかまいません。

1. Imagine that you have been diagnosed with HIV and told you have one month left to live. How would you spend your remaining time? What would you want the people around you to do?

_____

_____

_____

_____

2. Imagine that your friend has been diagnosed with HIV and told they have one month left to live. How would you react? Would you try to distance yourself from your friend or would you stay by them until the end?

_____

_____

_____

_____

Dallas Buyers Club（2013）
『ダラス・バイヤーズクラブ』

実話をもとにした本作は、第86回アカデミー賞で作品賞・脚本賞など6部門に
ノミネートされ、実在の人物ロン・ウッドルーフを演じたマシュー・マコノヒーが
主演男優賞を、トランスジェンダーのレイヨンを演じたジャレッド・レトが助演
男優賞を受賞した。

Column | HIV/AIDS と偏見

　HIV（Human Immunodeficiency Virus）は AIDS（Acquired Immune Deficiency Syndrome：
後天性免疫不全症候群）を発症させるヒト免疫不全ウイルスである。AIDS に感染すると免
疫力が低下して免疫不全状態に陥り、健康時にはかからないような重い感染症や悪性腫瘍
を発症し、あるいは痴呆や運動障害などの神経症状をきたし、適切な治療を受けなければ
死に至る。1981年にアメリカで最初の AIDS 患者が報告され、1983年にフランスのパスツー
ル研究所で HIV が発見された。2017年の時点で世界に約3,700万人の HIV 感染者がおり、
毎年約100万人が亡くなり、200万人が新たに感染しているという。

　アメリカで AIDS が広く知られるようになったのは、1985年にハリウッドの大物二枚目
スターであるロック・ハドソンが AIDS を発症していることと同性愛者であることを公に
したことによる。彼は同年に AIDS で他界したが、男らしいイメージの俳優として知られ
ていたため、同性愛者であるという告白は世間に大きな衝撃を与えた。本作の主人公であ
るロンが自分が HIV に感染していることを信じられなかったのも、ハドソンの新聞記事を
読んで「AIDS 患者＝同性愛者」と考えていたからである。

　日本で AIDS が広く知られるようになったのは「薬害エイズ事件」を通してである。
1980年代に血友病（血を固める「血液凝固因子」が足りないために出血すると簡単には止
まらない病気）の治療に使用された血液製剤の原料に、HIV に感染していたと推定される
外国の供血者からの血液が使われたことで多くの血友病患者がAIDSに罹患した。その結果、
日本の血友病患者の約4割にあたる1,800人が HIV に感染し、約600人以上が亡くなった
と伝えられている。

　ロンは自らの力で AIDS を治すべく、医学雑誌を読み漁って AIDS に効果のある薬を見
つけ出し、メキシコの医師から非合法なやり方で入手する。この未承認の薬を「ダラス・バ
イヤーズクラブ」という会員制のクラブを立ち上げて会員に配布する計画を練るのだが、
ネックになるのがロンが同性愛者を嫌悪するホモフォビア（homophobia）であるという点
である。AIDS 患者の多くが男性の同性愛者なのだが、彼には同性愛者のコネクションがな
い。そこで、ロンは自分と同じ病院で AIDS の治療を受けているトランスジェンダーのレ
イヨンをビジネスパートナーに引き入れることを思いつく。レイヨンは資金繰りが苦しく
なったロンを助けるべく、絶縁していた資産家の父のもとに金を借りに行く。これがきっ
かけとなり、ロンはレイヨンに対して深い友情を抱くようになり、ついにはレイヨンを抱
擁するに至るのである。

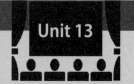

Unit 13

Finding a Cure

"American Sniper"

社会には様々な原因により PTSD（心的外傷後ストレス障害）に苦しんでいる人がいます。*American Sniper* の主人公で実在の狙撃兵であった Chris Kyle の場合はイラク戦争での体験が原因でした。

©Collection Christophel

 Key Vocabulary Match-up  DL 108   CD2-38

次の 1 ～ 5 の意味に合うものを a ～ e から選びましょう。

1. essence	( )	**a.**	not serving any purpose
2. regret	( )	**b.**	the cause of another event or act
3. trigger	( )	**c.**	the most basic property of something
4. useless	( )	**d.**	someone who has suffered due to something
5. victim	( )	**e.**	a feeling of wishing to have done something differently

次の文を読みましょう。

You lie silently on a rooftop, surveying the landscape beneath you. Your comrades are on the ground, looking for enemies. A suspicious man holding a metallic object is approaching them from behind—it's a bomb! You shoot
5　him in the head and save your comrades from being blown up. You are a hero. This is not a video game; it is reality for soldiers at war. Each action they take can potentially save or end a life, sometimes many. With so many dramatic experiences, many soldiers find themselves afflict-
10　ed with PTSD (Post-Traumatic Stress Disorder). This is a psychological condition resulting from a shocking experience, such as violence or immorality, which violates one's expectations of how the world should be. *American Sniper*'s protagonist, Chris Kyle, also a victim of this condi-
15　tion, reveals a ray of hope when he manages to find a cure.

In Iraq, Chris was a superb sniper. With remarkable accuracy, he took out many hostiles before they had a chance to kill his comrades. However, Chris fails to save
20　an informant as he and his children were tortured and killed, and this became a lasting trauma for him. After he returns home, he often appears to be spaced-out or cold to his wife—much of this time he is reliving this event and others from the war in his head. At one point, he attacks
25　a friendly dog which was licking his daughter because he confused it with the ferocious war canines he saw in Iraq. As his wife claims, his body was home, but his mind was still at war.

What finally allows him to overcome his trauma and
30　bring his mind home is not revenge or some great success on the battlefront. Talking to a doctor, he discovers the essence of his trauma. The biggest regret for him is having not been able to save more comrades. Furthermore,

comrade 同僚、同志

afflict 苦しめる

PTSD
　心的外傷後ストレス障害

immorality 不道徳（行為）

ray of hope 希望の光

informant 情報提供者

spaced-out ぼんやりする

ferocious どう猛な
canine イヌ

battlefront 前線、戦線

his skills seem useless in terms of raising a family. The
35 doctor introduces him to injured veterans in need of support at home. Chris begins to talk to them regularly and
help them to live more satisfying lives. This finally gives
him the moral justification to bring his mind home and
move beyond his trauma. What he needed was not to for-
40 get his experiences in Iraq, but to find a way to utilize
them at home.

A large number of war veterans contract PTSD, making their reintegration into mainstream society difficult.
Sadly, a majority are treated with no real success. Any
45 sufferer of PTSD, such as victims of parental abuse, rape,
natural disasters such as large earthquakes, or anyone
who has been a victim of extraordinary violence or pain,
may suffer from dilemmas like Chris. Triggers unexpect-
ed even to the individual can cause sudden violent out-
50 bursts in public, such as the friendly neighborhood dog
for Chris. Indeed, such unpredictable outbursts can make
them seem like scary individuals, but they are not "broken" individuals. Like Chris, many PTSD victims are
well-meaning, highly-capable individuals who have the
55 potential to contribute a great deal to the world.

American Sniper suggests that the solution may not
be to treat PTSD victims like disabled or broken individuals but to help them find the source of their trauma and
find a way to use it to make valuable contributions to so-
60 ciety. In the end, we all need to feel like we are needed; we
want to use our strengths to accomplish something mean-
ingful. Just as the doctor helped Chris find a way to apply
his, we could all work to provide opportunities for war
veterans and other victims of PTSD to apply their unique
65 experiences to help society.

in terms of ...
…の点では、…に関して

justification 正当化

reintegration
再統合、復帰

outburst 爆発

highly-capable
非常に有能な

Comprehension Check

Read & Write

次の質問が本文の内容に合えば T（True）を、合わなければ F（False）を選びましょう。
また、その理由を本文から抜き出してみましょう。

1. A failure at the battlefront caused a trauma for Chris.　　　　T / F

Why?: _____

2. Chris felt it was morally acceptable for him to live a normal life at home.　T / F

Why?: _____

3. Often even the PTSD victim does not know what will trigger their disease.

　　　　　　　　　　　　　　　　　　　　　　　　　　　　　　T / F

Why?: _____

Listen & Write 　　　 🎧 DL 114~116　 ◉ CD2-44 ～ ◉ CD2-46

音声を聞いて空所を埋めてから、本文の内容に最も合うものを選びましょう。

1. _____ of the following is a potential _____ of PTSD?
(A) DNA damage
(B) An unhealthy diet
(C) Parental violence
(D) Touching someone with PTSD

2. _____ would Chris's wife describe him after _____
_____?
(A) A dedicated father
(B) A great soldier
(C) A distant person
(D) A cruel husband

3. _____ did Chris's mind need to _____ _____ PTSD?
(A) A doctor
(B) A purpose
(C) Better morals
(D) A loving family

Write & Speak

次の語句の意味を英英辞典で調べて書いてみましょう。その後で、ペアを組んで相手に説明してみましょう。

A: "cure" means

B: "trauma" means

🎥 Thinking about Our Diversity

次の質問について考えて、自分の意見を書いてみましょう。ペアやグループで話し合ってもかまいません。

1. Imagine that you are suffering from PTSD. Now think of a cause for it. What would you do to face the cause? Also, how would you want the people around you to treat you?

_____

_____

_____

_____

2. Imagine that your acquaintance is suffering from PTSD. How would you act around them?

_____

_____

_____

_____

American Sniper（2014）
『アメリカン・スナイパー』

イラク戦争時、「伝説の狙撃手」と呼ばれたアメリカの狙撃兵クリス・カイルの自伝を原作とする本作。第87回アカデミー賞では作品賞など6部門にノミネートされ、カイル役のブラッドリー・クーパーも主演男優賞にノミネートされた。

| Column | 戦争とPTSD |

　PTSD（Post-Traumatic Stress Disorder）とは「心的外傷後ストレス障害」と呼ばれる心理障害であり、1980年代、ベトナム戦争からの帰還兵が社会復帰後に深刻な心理障害を示して問題となったことから研究されるようになった。1990年の調査によれば、従軍経験のある315万人の兵士および将校の約15パーセントがPTSDに悩まされているとのことである。2014年には1日平均20人の元兵士が自殺し、そのうち65パーセントが50歳以上で、大半がベトナム戦争に従軍していたと言われている。また、アメリカがアフガニスタンおよびイラクに派遣した兵士を調査したデイヴィッド・フィンケルの『帰還兵はなぜ自殺するのか』（亜紀書房）によれば、派兵された200万人のうち50万人にPTSDの症状がみられるという。そのうちの1人が『アメリカン・スナイパー』の主人公である「伝説の狙撃手」クリス・カイル（1974-2013）である。

　テキサスで生まれ育ったカイルは、当初はカウボーイになることを目指し、ロデオに熱中してプロの競技者となる。しかし、腕を負傷したことと、1998年にケニアとタンザニアで起こったアメリカ大使館爆破事件の惨状を目にしたことがきっかけとなり、軍人へと進路を変更する。海軍に入隊したカイルは過酷な訓練に耐え、海軍特殊部隊Navy SEALs（ネイビーシールズ）の一員となり、2003年のイラク戦争開戦以降、4回出征する。

　彼が「伝説の狙撃手」と呼ばれ、また敵であるイラク側からは激戦地の名を取って「ラマーディーの悪魔」（Devil of Ramadi）と呼ばれて懸賞金をかけられるほど恐れられたのは、米軍史上最多の160人を射殺したことに加えて、1.9キロメートル離れた標的を撃ち抜く狙撃の精度によるところも大きい。彼の常人離れした狙撃の精度は、オリンピックのメダリストである敵兵を狙撃する本作の場面を見れば納得できるであろう。

　除隊後、カイルは民間の軍事会社を創業し、またPTSDに苦しむ帰還兵や退役兵の社会復帰を支援するNPO団体を設立した。さらに、本作の原作となる自らの戦争体験を綴った回想録を出版するなど精力的に活動していたが、2013年、PTSDを患う元海兵隊員を訪問した際に発砲され、命を落としている。

Unit 14

— Refugees

Is Your World Peaceful?

"Hotel Rwanda"

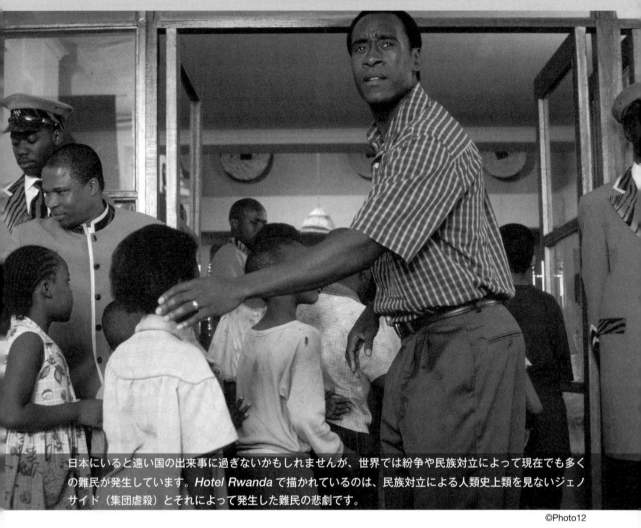

日本にいると遠い国の出来事に過ぎないかもしれませんが、世界では紛争や民族対立によって現在でも多くの難民が発生しています。*Hotel Rwanda* で描かれているのは、民族対立による人類史上類を見ないジェノサイド（集団虐殺）とそれによって発生した難民の悲劇です。

©Photo12

Key Vocabulary Match-up　 DL 117　CD2-47

次の 1 ～ 5 の意味に合うものを a ～ e から選びましょう。

1. candidate　　(　)　　**a.** a very sad event
2. conflict　　　(　)　　**b.** to be a danger to something
3. ignore　　　 (　)　　**c.** purposely not notice something
4. threaten　　 (　)　　**d.** disagreement often involving violence
5. tragedy　　　(　)　　**e.** something which can possibly fill a certain role

次の文を読みましょう。

For many of us, it may seem that we are living in a relatively peaceful world, but how much of the earth does such a world contain? Refugee camps are one clear instance of something it does not. Refugees are people who
5 have had to flee their homes due to threat of violence. In countries like Japan, where very few living people have direct experience with such conflict, these victims can seem almost like the fictional characters we see in movies. Nevertheless, they are a real tragedy existing on the
10 earth. *Hotel Rwanda*, the story of Rwandan refugees who were nearly slaughtered by their own countrypeople, invites us to expand our world by giving a raw portrayal of the refugee situation.

Paul Rusesabagina, a Rwandan, is the manager of a
15 high-class hotel. A Hutu, he is on the strong side of a socio-ethnic national divide with the Tutsi. His wife being a Tutsi, he clearly does not support this divide. Nevertheless, when his Tutsi neighbors are assaulted by the anti-Tutsi militia, he watches passively, though disgustedly,
20 claiming that he must save his resources for his own family. However, the very next day he comes home from work to find many of his Tutsi neighbors hiding in his house. When he asks his wife why they came to him for help and not others, his wife tells him that he is the only one who
25 can prevent them from being killed. Knowing that if he does not act the people in front of him will die, he is charged with a personal responsibility—he resolves to help them to take refuge at his hotel.

Outside the hotel, a genocide of all Tutsi proceeds in
30 full throttle. Throughout the country, Tutsi are slaughtered and killed in their homes by their former neighbors with no forewarning or hesitation. Since any Tutsi that steps even a foot outside the hotel premises will be slaugh-

Rwanda ルワンダ
　（東アフリカの共和国）
slaughter 虐殺する
countrypeople 同国人
portrayal 肖像、描写

Hutu フツ（ツチ、トゥワ
　とともにルワンダとブル
　ンジに住む民族）
socio-ethnic
　社会民族的な
Tutsi ツチ
anti-Tutsi militia
　反ツチ軍
disgustedly
　うんざりしたように

genocide
　大虐殺、集団虐殺
in full throttle
　全開で、最高潮で

forewarning
　前もって警告する

tered, Paul must make trips outside to procure food and
35 supplies for the refugees. In the process, his vehicle must
literally drive over a pile of hundreds of Tutsi corpses cov-
ering the road. In Paul's world, there is no peace.

For the refugees, what seemed like a relatively peaceful world became a menacing place which threatens their
40 lives overnight. They seek desperately for help and, since
their enemies are their own countrypeople, the only can-
didates are other countries. But, is it reasonable to hope
that other countries intervene? This is where a couple of
reporters from the US come into play. They have captured
45 footage of the slaughter and Paul thanks them, believing
that other countries would come to help if they saw the
atrocities. To this, one of the reporters replies:

"I think if people see this footage they'll say, "oh my
God that's horrible," and then go on eating their din-
50 ners."

For the majority of us, this is exactly true. Since we only
see such problems on television, it is easy to disregard
them and return to our peaceful world.

When a person's situation is closer to our heart, per-
55 haps because it is physically closer or perhaps because we
have related experiences, it is much harder to ignore. For
example, someone who was bullied as a child will be likely to help a child they see being bullied while someone
who has not been bullied will often look the other way. We
60 should certainly hope that the refugee situation will never be so close to us, but *Hotel Rwanda* offers us a chance
to see a darker part of our planet without actually going
there. If we can all include a little bit more of the earth in
what we include in our everyday worlds, we may soon find
65 ourselves on an earth much closer to peace than now.

procure 入手する

corpse 死体

menacing
　恐ろしい、脅威を与える

come into play 関与する

footage フィルム映像

atrocity 残虐行為

Comprehension Check

Read & Write

次の質問が本文の内容に合えば T（True）を、合わなければ F（False）を選びましょう。
また、その理由を本文から抜き出してみましょう。

1. Our experiences influence how we view refugees.　　　　　　T / F

　Why?: _____

2. The only possible hope for the Rwandan refugees is foreigners.　　T / F

　Why?: _____

3. Most people would want to help the refugees if they knew the situation. T / F

　Why?: _____

Listen & Write　　　　　　　　　　　DL 123~125　　CD2-53 ~ CD2-55

音声を聞いて空所を埋めてから、本文の内容に最も合うものを選びましょう。

1. _____ is most likely to have a _____ _____?

　(A) A person who belongs to the United Nations

　(B) A person living near Rwanda

　(C) A person who is friends with someone from Africa

　(D) A person who lives in Japan

2. _____ do we first know that Paul does not _____ the Tutsi?

　(A) His hotel

　(B) His wife

　(C) His actions

　(D) His ethnicity

3. According to this essay, _____ might we start _____ the _____ more peaceful?

　(A) Watch more international movies

　(B) Think more about distant places

　(C) Get closer to the refugee situation

　(D) Join an international organization like the United Nations

Write & Speak

次の語句の意味を英英辞典で調べて書いてみましょう。その後で、ペアを組んで相手に説明してみましょう。

> **A:** "refugee" means

> **B:** "peace" means

🎥 Thinking about Our Diversity

次の質問について考えて、自分の意見を書いてみましょう。ペアやグループで話し合ってもかまいません。

1. Imagine that a large conflict has started in your country and you are now a refugee. What would you do? Where would you go to escape?

   _____

   _____

   _____

   _____

2. Imagine that you are eating dinner and see the horrible situation of some refugees on the news. How would you feel? Would you decide it is none of your concern? Is there anything you think you could or should do?

   _____

   _____

   _____

   _____

Hotel Rwanda（2004）
『ホテル・ルワンダ』

1994年のルワンダ虐殺を描いた本作で、1,200人以上の難民をホテルに匿い命を救った実在のホテルマンであるポール・ルセサバギナ（写真右）を演じたドン・チードルは、第77回アカデミー賞で主演男優賞にノミネートされた。ルセサバギナはその行動から「アフリカのシンドラー」と呼ばれている。

Column ルワンダの歴史と虐殺

　第二次世界大戦以前、アメリカから移住したアフリカ系解放奴隷が建国したリベリアを除いて、アフリカ諸国はすべてヨーロッパ列強諸国の植民地支配を受けていた。現在のルワンダ共和国は、1899年にドイツ領東アフリカの一部となるまで、牧畜中心に生業を営む少数派のツチ（Tutsi）が農耕中心で多数派のフツ（Hutu）を支配するルワンダ王国であった。第一次世界大戦後はベルギーの統治領となったが、ベルギーは既存の統治機構を利用する間接統治政策をおこなった。その結果、ツチの権力は温存され、フツを支配する中間支配層に据えられた。

　1957年、ツチによる長年の支配に不満を抱くフツの知識人による「バフツ宣言」によって、ツチの専制終結と植民地体制打破が宣言された。59年に国王ムタラ3世が死去すると、ベルギー当局とツチの関係が悪化し、同年11月にはフツが決起して騒乱が全国に広がっていった。61年、ベルギー当局はクーデターによって軍政を敷いて王制を廃止し、翌年7月1日にはルワンダ共和国が誕生してフツのグレゴワール・カイバンダが初代大統領に就任した。カイバンダ政権下ではフツによるツチに対する暴力が事実上容認され、ツチは政治の表舞台から排斥された。

　その後、90年にはツチ系難民によって結成された反政府武装組織であるルワンダ愛国戦線（RPF: Rwanda Patriotic Front）とルワンダ政府との戦闘が始まった。これがルワンダ紛争である。93年8月、隣国タンザニアのアルーシャで和平合意が締結されたが、翌年4月6日、フツ出身の第2代大統領ハビャリマナが乗っていた飛行機が何者かに撃墜され死亡したことで、フツ過激派の民兵組織が中心になってツチやフツ穏健派に対する虐殺が勃発した。『ホテル・ルワンダ』はこの「ルワンダ虐殺」の前夜から始まる。

　虐殺はルワンダ愛国戦線が大攻勢をかけて本土を掌握し、新政府を樹立することで終焉した。94年4月からの約100日間で、当時のルワンダの総人口約730万人のうちおよそ80〜100万人が虐殺の犠牲になったと推測されている。第二次世界大戦中の1939年から45年にかけておこなわれたナチス・ドイツによるユダヤ人大虐殺は600万人を超えると推定されているが、ルワンダ虐殺の死亡率はその2.9〜3.6倍に匹敵するものである。一夜にして約4万5千人が虐殺された技術学校の跡地には、現在、ムランビ虐殺記念館が建っている。

Unit 15

Sense of Reason
"Schindler's List"

ホロコーストは人類がどこまで理性を失い残虐になれるかを示す歴史的事実です。なぜ人間はある人種を差別し虐げるのでしょうか。私たちはどうすれば歴史から学ぶことができるでしょうか。*Schindler's List* の主人公 Oskar Schindler のケースを見てみましょう。

©Photo12

 Key Vocabulary Match-up　　 DL 126　◉ CD2-56

次の１～５の意味に合うものをａ～ｅから選びましょう。

1. consequence	( )	**a.** a particular understanding of something
2. genocide	( )	**b.** a particular way of accomplishing something
3. procedure	( )	**c.** a fact which shows that something is true
4. proof	( )	**d.** murder targeted at an entire group of people
5. sense	( )	**e.** something that results because of something else

次の文を読みましょう。

　　Procedures are an important part of society. A good procedure clearly lists the steps to successfully achieve a goal. Going to work or school every day, resting on the weekend, eating three meals a day, these everyday ac-
5 tions are actually part of a procedure to achieve a fulfilling life. Since everyone takes their validity for granted, we tend to follow them without much thought. However, sometimes procedures are created based on unsound reasoning. If we blindly follow these, the results can be disas-
10 trous. *Schindler's List* depicts the Holocaust, an unspeakably horrendous example of human genocide made into a procedure, and the miracle of a man who overcame it by maintaining his sense of reason.

　　Morals can only inform our behavior when we think
15 about the consequences; Nazi Germany enacted the Holocaust by separating reason from behavior. At the start of the movie, armbands are being distributed to Jewish people of all different lifestyles and manner of dress in order to make them into a visibly recognizable group. It was
20 clear and simple; people with armbands were less than human, they were enemies of Germany and they were to be purged. It became standard procedure and, with no reason to think for themselves whether hating Jewish Germans was right, soldiers, civilians, even children fol-
25 lowed. However, this only lasted as long as the Nazi government guaranteed the procedure. When it lost the war, the former Nazi guards had to think about their actions again and they stopped their hate crimes very quickly.

　　On the other hand, protagonist Oskar Schindler was
30 a man who never gave up his sense of reason. He was an opportunist seeking to use any resources available to get ahead of others. Thanks to the dangerous situation for all Jewish people, he could get investment from wealthy

unsound
不安定な、あやふやな

the Holocaust
ホロコースト（第二次世
界大戦におけるナチスに
よるユダヤ人の大虐殺）
horrendous 恐ろしい

enact
成立させる、制定する

purge 追放する

opportunist
日和見主義者
get ahead of ...
…の先を行く

Jewish people by promising them safety. Jewish labor
35 was also extremely cheap because no one else wanted it.
For his factory, Jews were valuable assets, not people,
judged purely in terms of their productivity. Just as we
discard a computer when it stops working, so would
Schindler discard a Jewish person. At least, that was the
40 plan.

Originally, Schindler indeed used the system for personal profit. However, each time a Jewish person thanked
him for saving his life, or he saw little Jewish girls dead
on the street, or a person begged him to save a life, he had
45 to think about the actions being carried out on humans,
not on armbands. This allowed his morals to surface. He
shifted from using the system for profit to using it to keep
the Jewish workers in his factory out of harm's way. For
example, though he never intended to make them do so,
50 he told Nazi soldiers that two little girls' small fingers
were essential to polish the inside of small shell casings.
They were allowed to go to his factory. Although one man
could never stop something as large as the Holocaust,
Schindler's sense of reason allowed him to recognize its
55 flaws and work within it, miraculously saving 1,200 lives.

Children angrily screaming "Goodbye, Jews!" at
trucks packed full of Jewish prisoners as they are driven
to their death. Soldiers shooting crying children and the
elderly. Hundreds of Jewish people made to strip naked in
60 public and run in lines. We would like to think that normal people are not capable of such things. Unfortunately,
the Holocaust is proof that, when procedure replaces reason as justification for an action, everyday people readily
become actors in systematic genocide. To prevent this
65 from happening, we must all strive to understand the
reasoning behind a procedure before following it. Then,
like Oskar Schindler, we might bring about our own miracle.

keep ... out of harm's way …が危害を受けないようにする

shell casing 薬きょう

flaw 欠陥

strip naked 全裸になる

Comprehension Check

Read & Write

次の質問が本文の内容に合えば T（True）を、合わなければ F（False）を選びましょう。
また、その理由を本文から抜き出してみましょう。

1. We follow some procedures because we thoughtlessly accept them as effective.

T / F

Why?: _____

2. Schindler's main goal until the end was to make money.　　　　T / F

Why?: _____

3. All people have the possibility of murdering if it fits a system.　　　T / F

Why?: _____

Listen & Write　　　　🎧 DL 132~134　◎ CD2-62 ~ ◎ CD2-64

音声を聞いて空所を埋めてから、本文の内容に最も合うものを選びましょう。

1. _____ did children and normal Germans _____ _____
_____ the Holocaust?
(A) The soldiers made them do it.
(B) They were too scared not to.
(C) It seemed normal.
(D) They thought hating Jewish people was right.

2. _____ was Schindler able to _____ Jewish _____ in
his factory at first?
(A) He kept it a secret.
(B) He treated them like tools.
(C) He used his political authority.
(D) He stayed outside Germany.

3. _____ did Schindler start using his factory to _____ the Jews?
(A) He fell in love with a Jewish girl.
(B) He saw that they were working too hard.
(C) He thought about how they were being treated.
(D) He stopped making a profit from the factory.

Write & Speak

次の語句の意味を英英辞典で調べて書いてみましょう。その後で、ペアを組んで相手に説明してみましょう。

> **A:** "hate crime" means

> **B:** "reason" means

🎥 Thinking about Our Diversity

次の質問について考えて、自分の意見を書いてみましょう。ペアやグループで話し合ってもかまいません。

1. Imagine you are suffering from prejudice just for being a certain ethnicity. How would you feel? How would you act in such a situation?

_____

_____

_____

_____

2. Imagine you are being forced to be prejudiced against a certain ethnic group. If you do not obey, you are also in danger. What would you do? Would you follow orders, or would you resist?

_____

_____

_____

_____

Schindler's List（1993）
『シンドラーのリスト』

第二次世界大戦におけるナチス・ドイツによるユダヤ人大虐殺（ホロコースト）から1,200人ものユダヤ人の命を救ったドイツ人実業家オスカー・シンドラーを描いた本作。第66回アカデミー賞では12部門にノミネートされ、作品賞・監督賞など7部門で受賞を果たし、自身もユダヤ系アメリカ人であるスティーブン・スピルバーグ監督に念願のオスカーをもたらした。

| Column | 日本の2人のシンドラー |

　ナチスによるユダヤ人迫害が始まったのはヒトラーが首相となった1933年とされている。その年、ヒトラーはユダヤ人の経営する商店や会社に対してボイコットを実行し、35年にはユダヤ人とドイツ人との結婚を禁じる「ドイツ人の血と名誉を守るための法律」や、ユダヤ人の公民権を喪失させる「帝国市民法」から成る「ニュルンベルク法」を制定した。40年になるとユダヤ人の迫害にさらに拍車がかかり、ヨーロッパ各地から送り込まれたユダヤ人がゲットー（ghetto）と呼ばれる監視付き居住区に収容されることになった。41年にはユダヤ人であることを示す黄色い星の印の着用が義務づけられることになり、抹殺を意味する「最終的解決」の準備命令が下った。『シンドラーのリスト』で描かれているのは、「最終的解決」の最終段階ともいえる43年から45年の物語である。

　本作の主人公オスカー・シンドラー（1908-74）に先立ち、ユダヤ人救出に尽力した2人の日本人がいる。1人は杉原千畝（1900-86）、もう1人は樋口季一郎（1888-1970）である。

　リトアニアの在カウナス領事館の領事代理に任命された杉原は、1940年7月、領事館に救いを求めてやって来た多くのユダヤ避難民に対し、本省の訓令に反して6,000人以上に「命のビザ」を発給したといわれている。彼はこの功績によって、「諸国民の中の正義の人」という称号を1985年に授与された。この称号は、ナチス・ドイツによるユダヤ人絶滅から自らの命の危険を冒してまでユダヤ人を守った非ユダヤ人に贈られるものである。

　樋口は現在の兵庫県南あわじ市に生まれ、陸軍幼年学校、陸軍士官学校、陸軍大学校を経て、1919年に大尉に昇進し陸軍参謀本部に勤務する。37年、少将に昇進し満州のハルピン特務機関長の任にあった樋口は、ソ連と満州の国境の町オトポールにたどり着いた多数

のユダヤ避難民が、満州への国境通過許可がもらえず命の危機にあることを知る。彼は当時の満州鉄道総裁であり後に外務大臣となる松岡洋右に直談判し、国境通過を認めさせた（オトポール事件）。この樋口の断行のおかげで、一説では2万人のユダヤ人が救われたといわれている。戦後、樋口を戦犯として裁くために引き渡しを要求したソ連のスターリンに対して、ユダヤ人会議は世界規模で樋口救出運動を展開した。その結果、マッカーサーはソ連からの引き渡し要求を拒否し、彼の身柄を保護したのであった。

本書には音声CD（別売）があります

Our Society, Our Diversity, Our Movies
映画に観る多文化社会のかたち

2020年1月20日　初版第1刷発行
2023年9月10日　初版第8刷発行

編著者　　Joseph Tabolt
　　　　　森　永　弘　司

発行者　　福　岡　正　人
発行所　　株式会社　金星堂

〒101-0051 東京都千代田区神田神保町 3-21
Tel. （03）3263-3828（営業部）
　　 （03）3263-3997（編集部）
Fax （03）3263-0716
https://www.kinsei-do.co.jp

編集担当／今門貴浩　　　　　　　Printed in Japan
印刷・製本所／萩原印刷株式会社

ISBN978-4-7647-4101-0　C1082